A Bonne Vie Book | Bonne Vie, Orlando, Florida
www.BonneVie.store

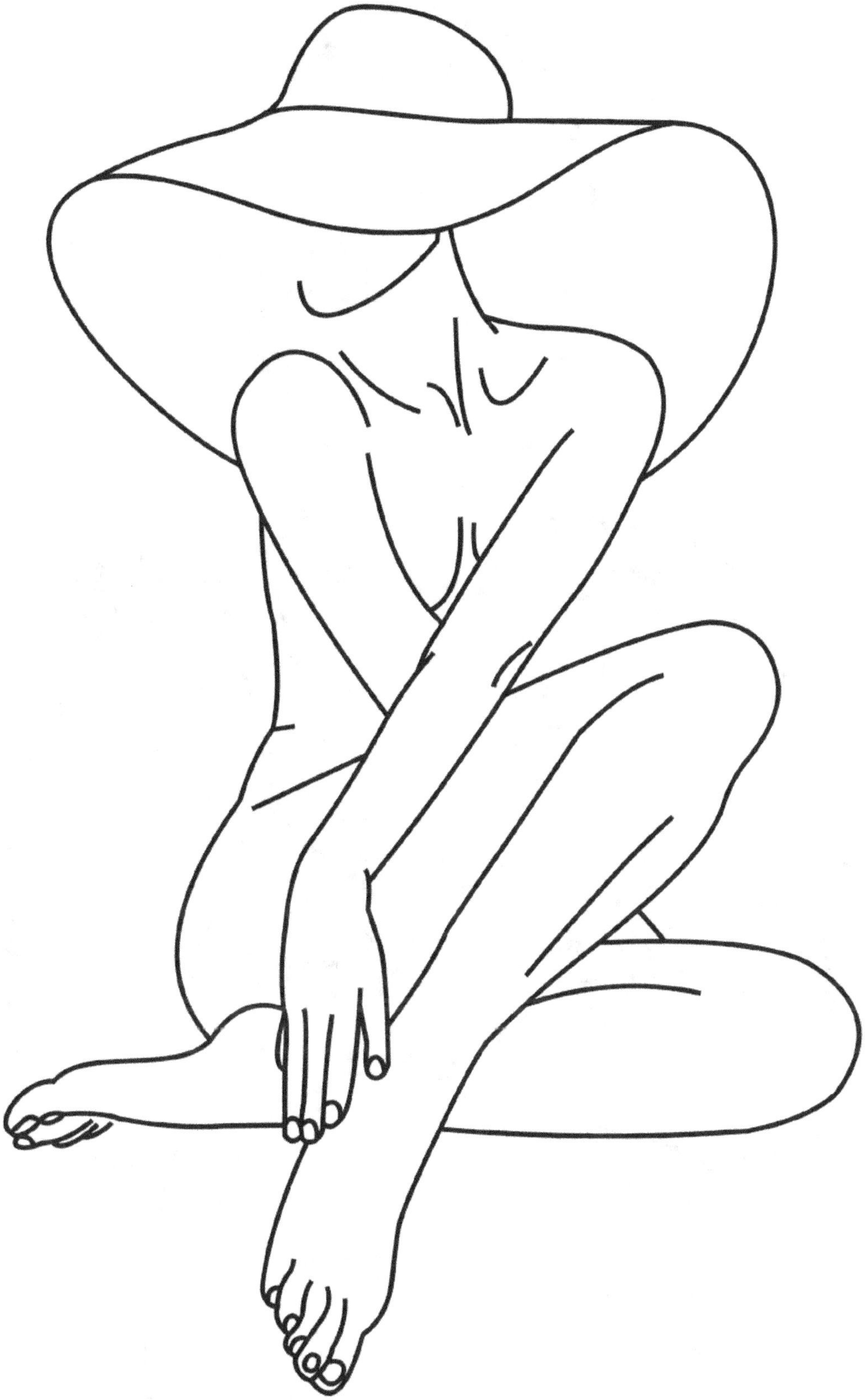

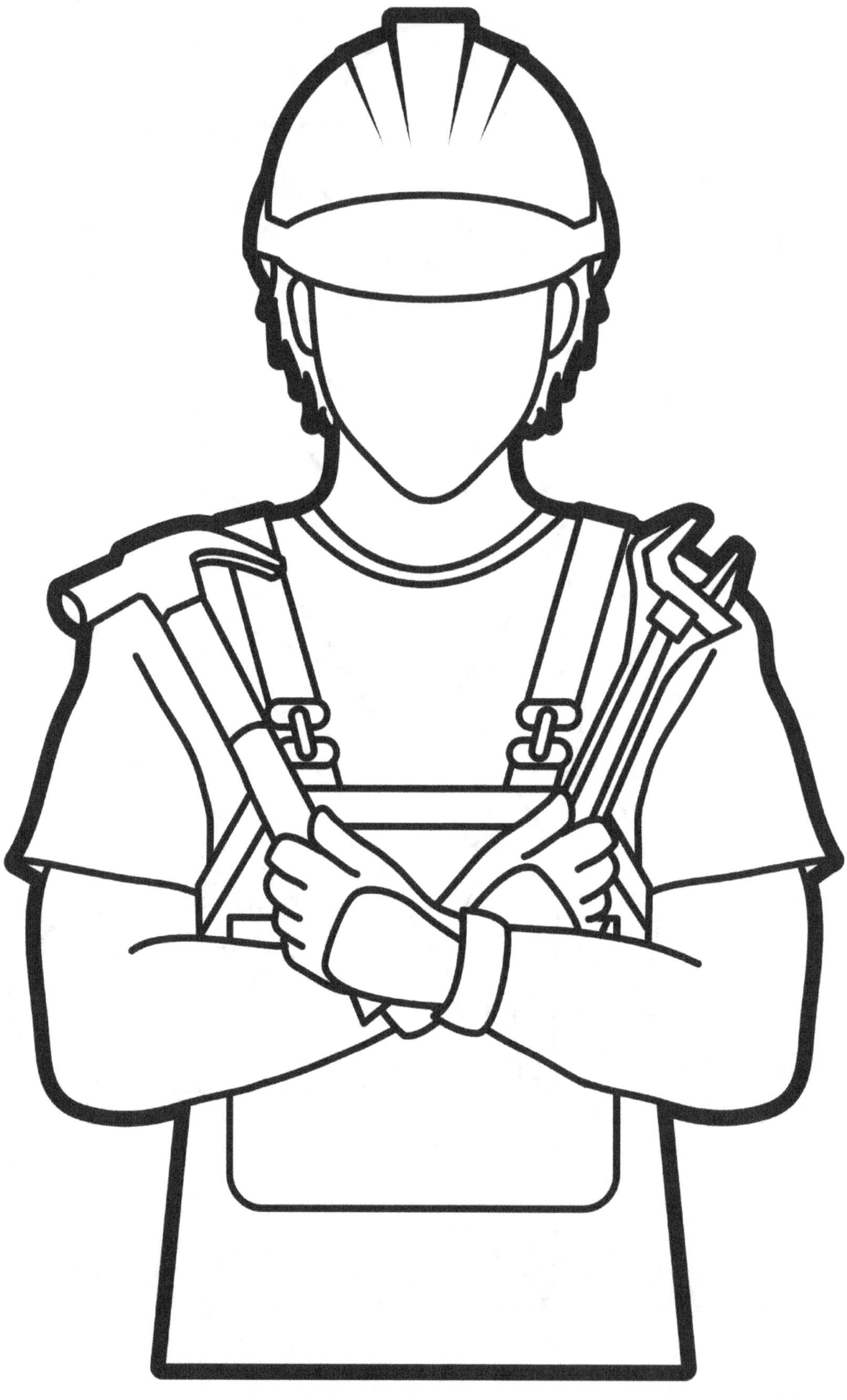

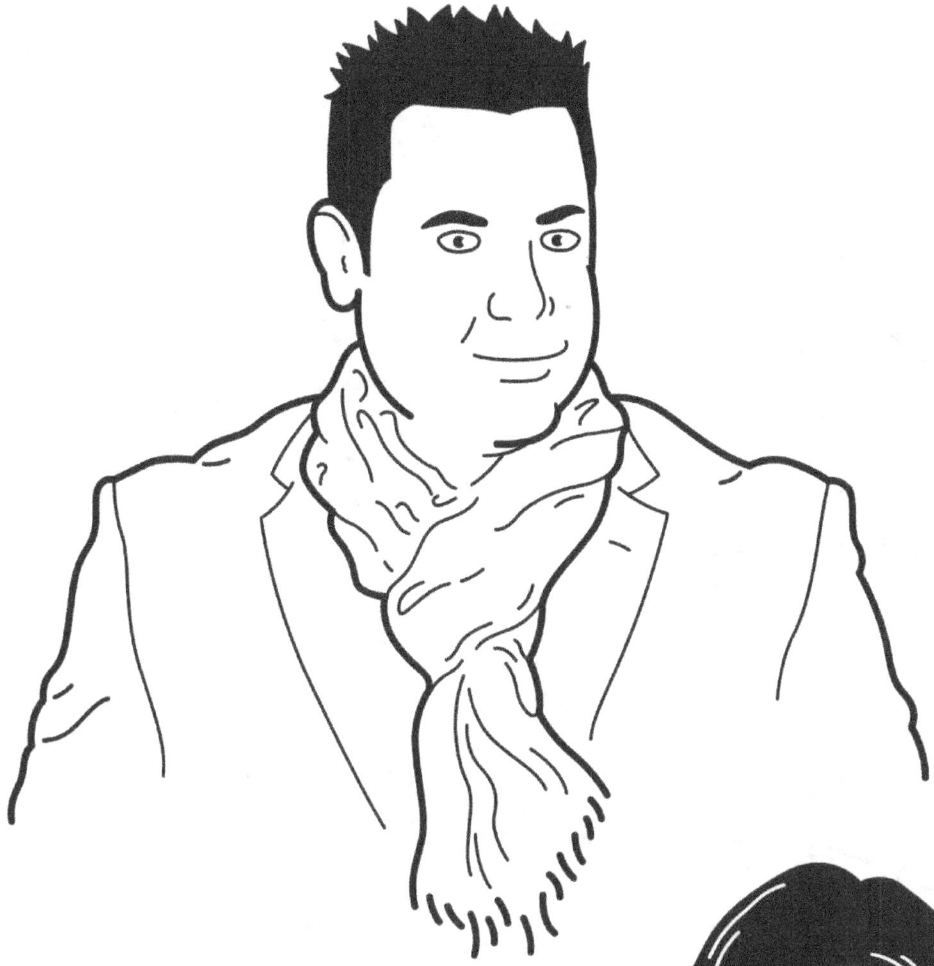
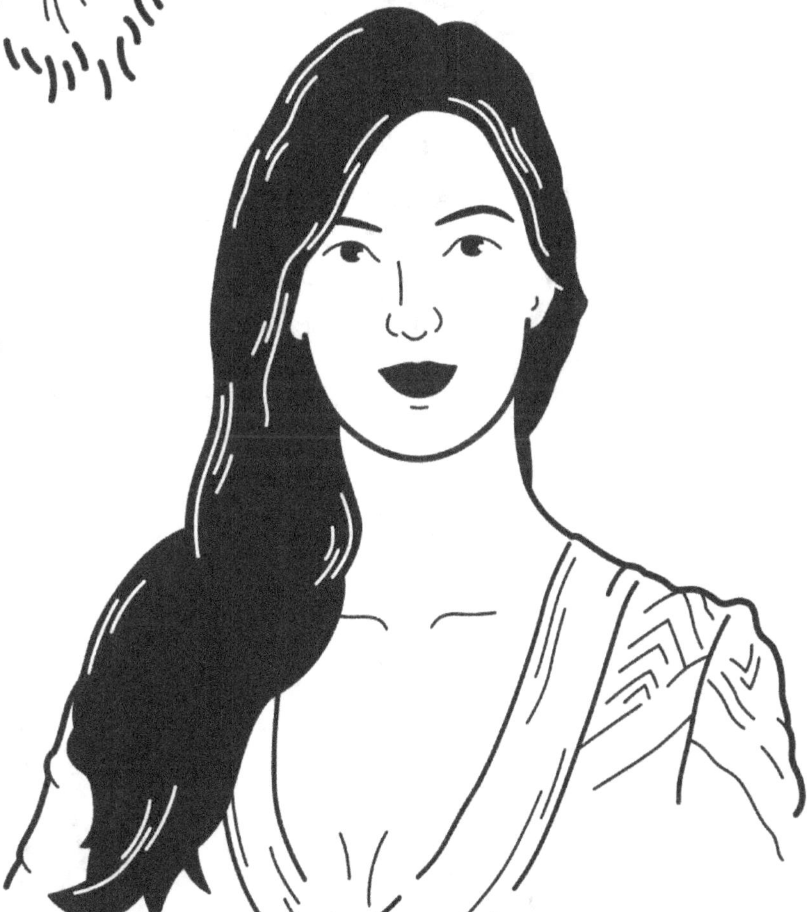

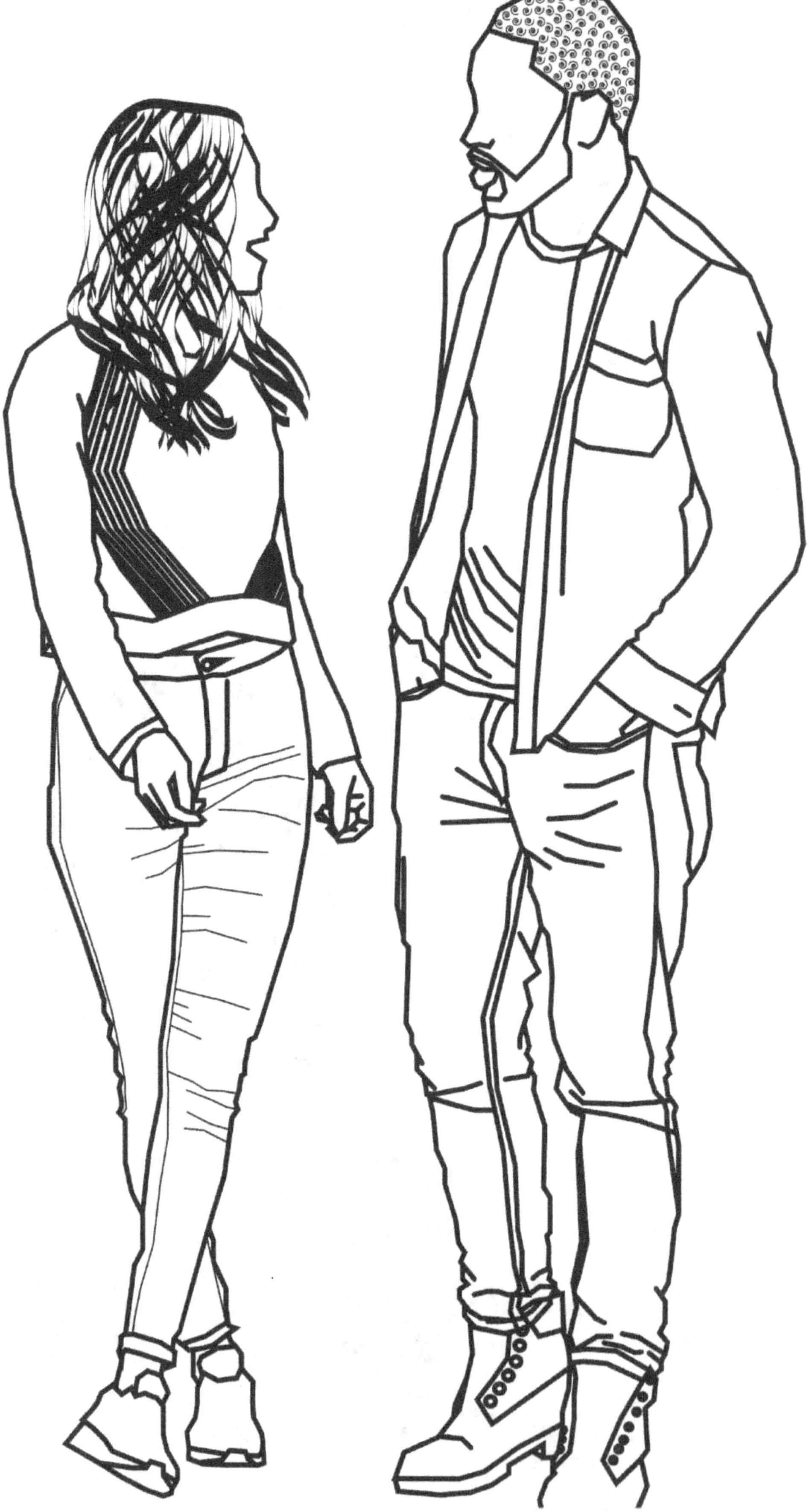

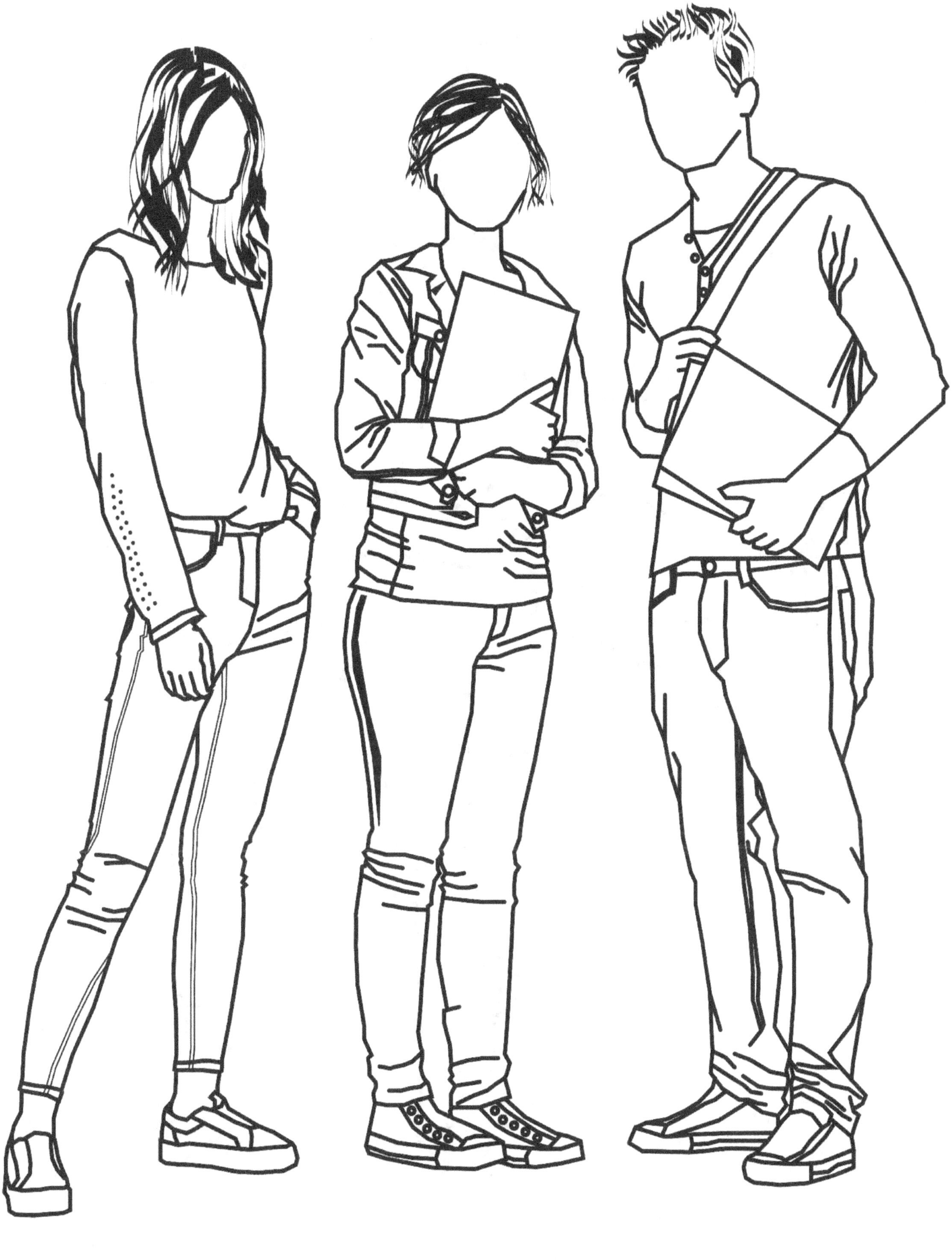

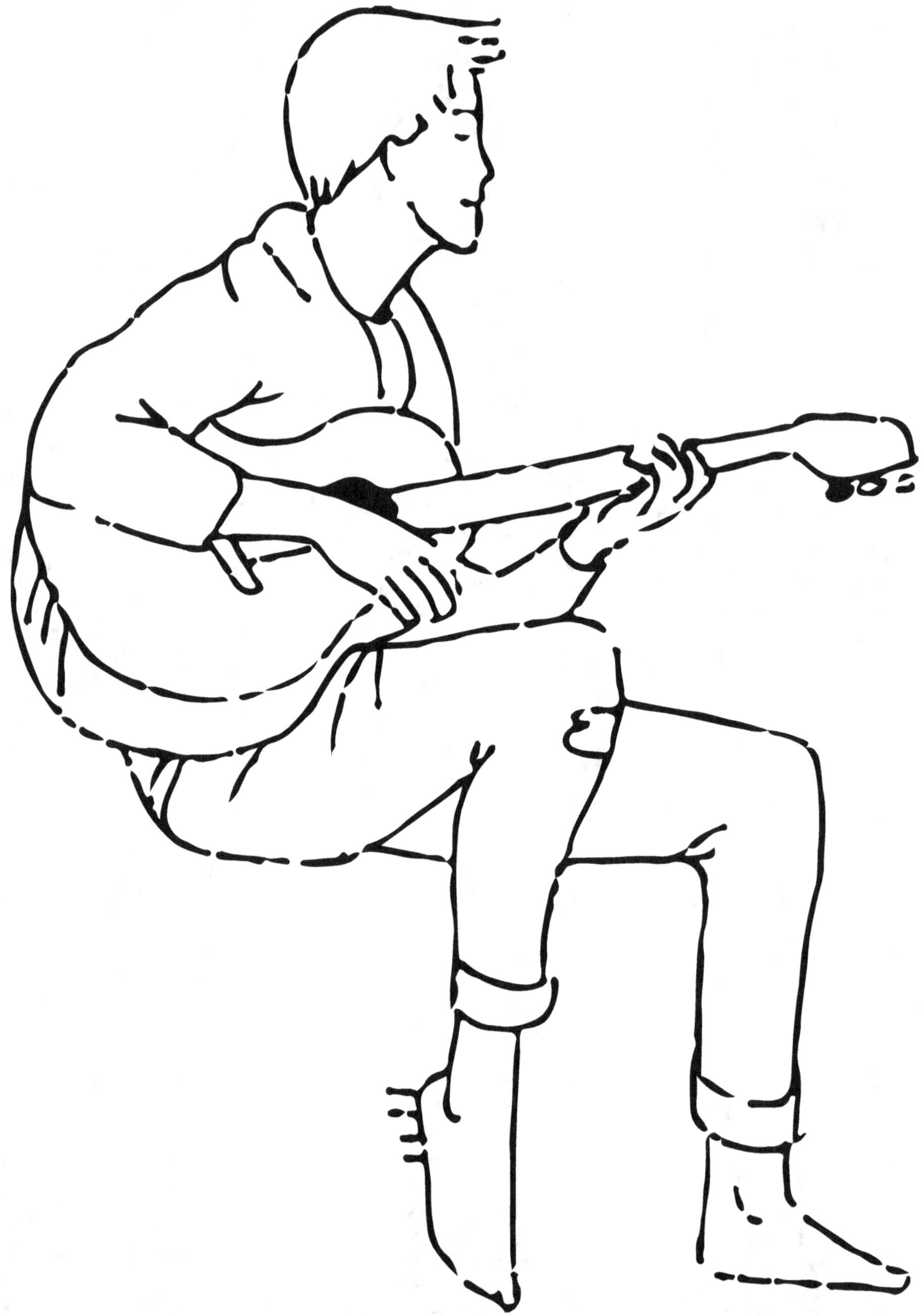

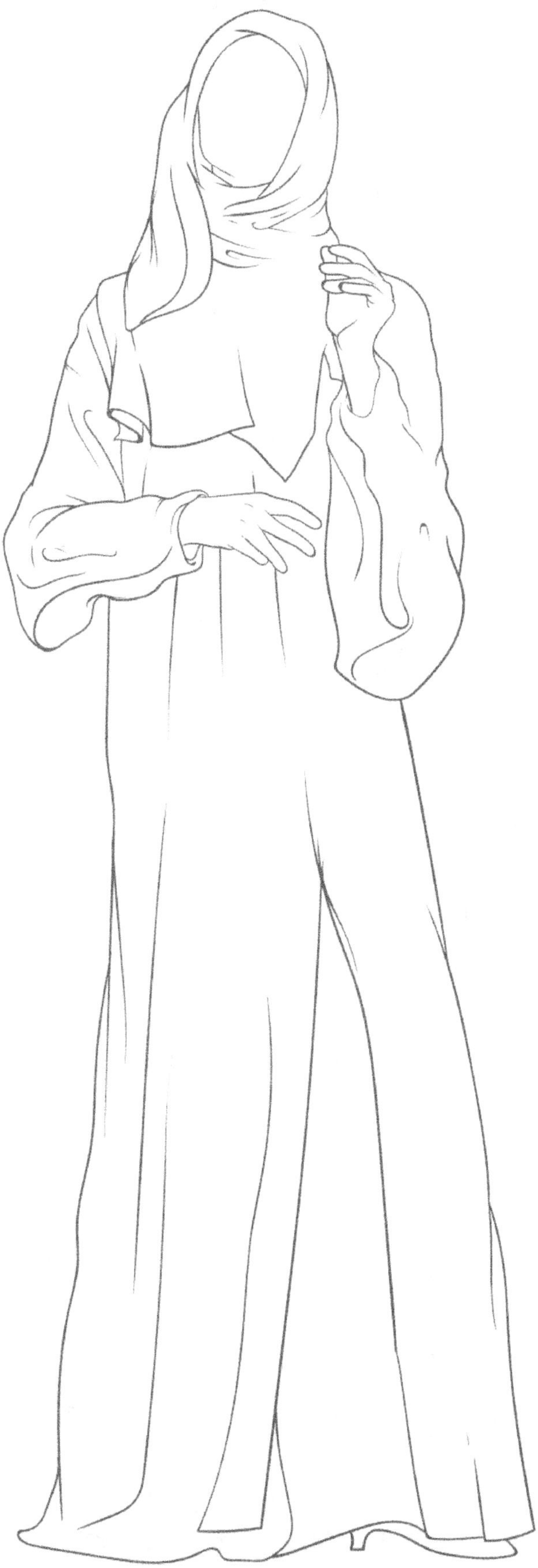

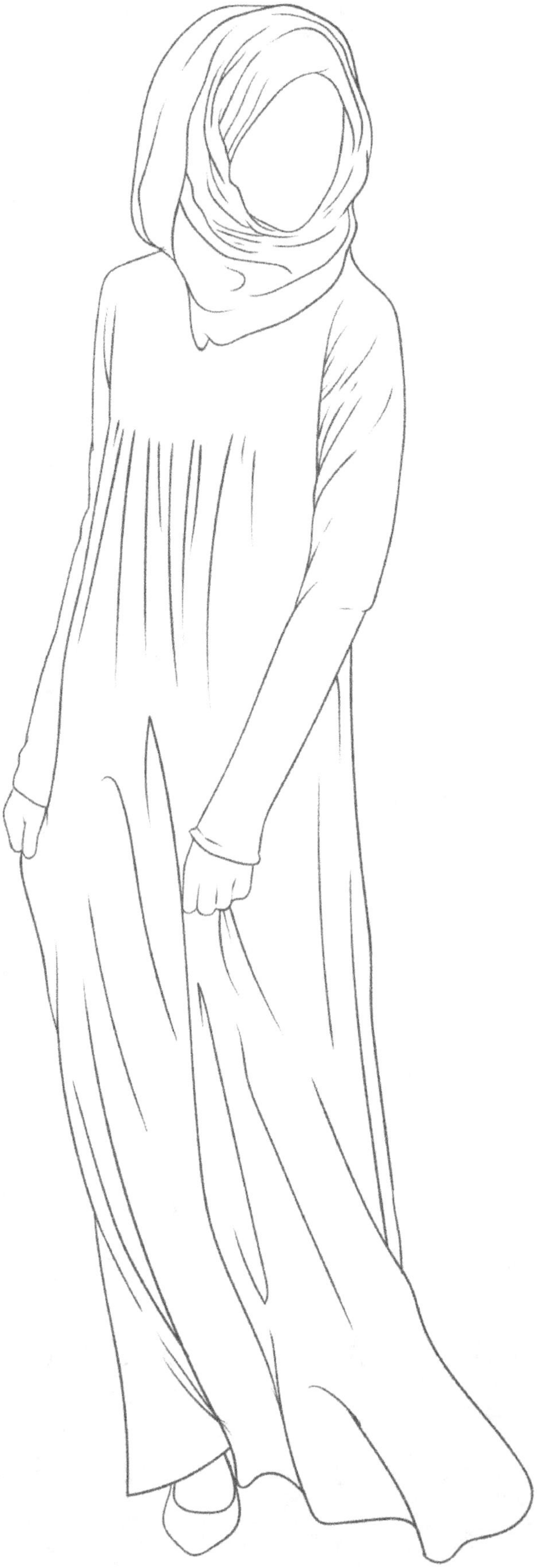

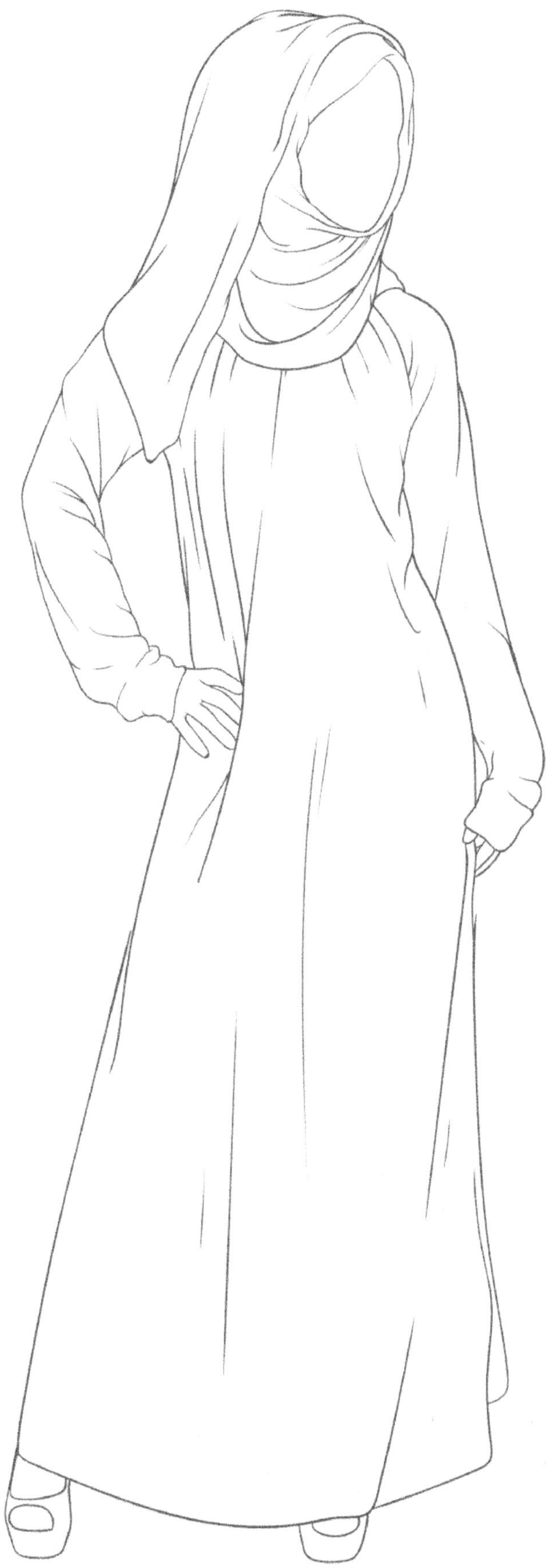

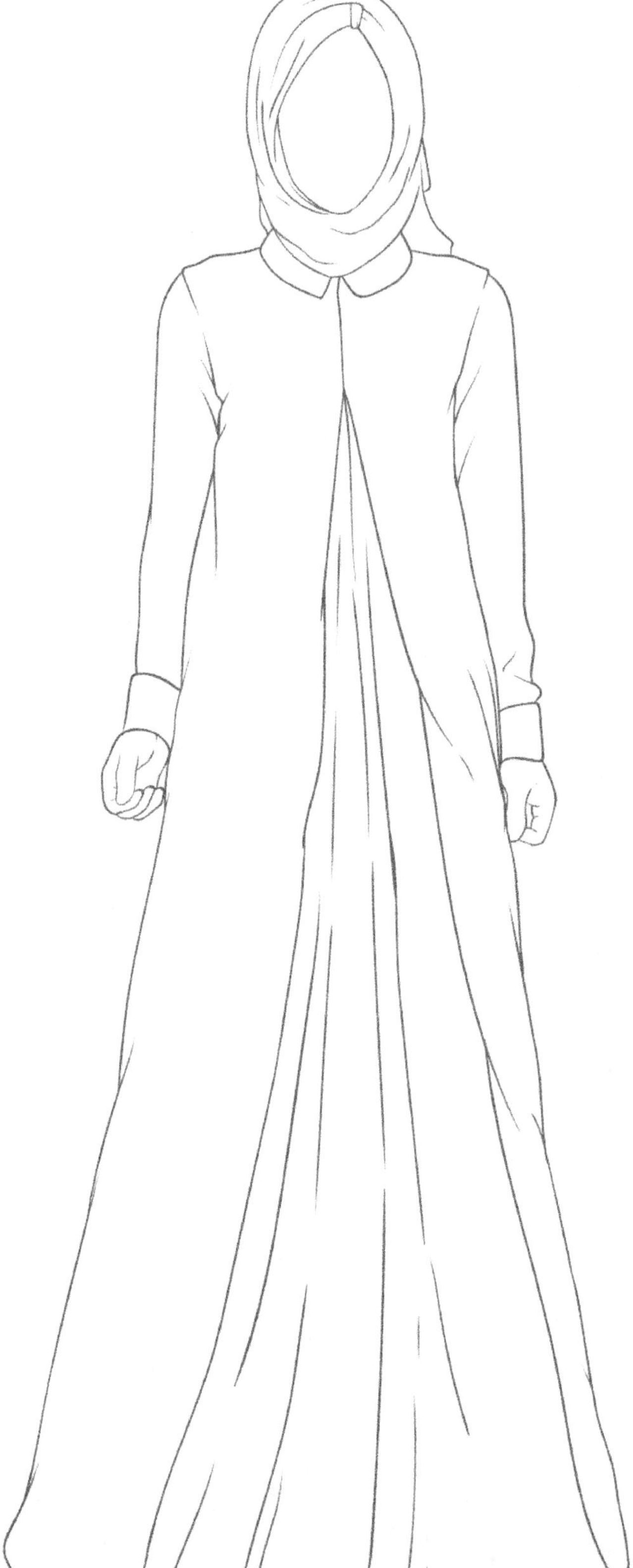

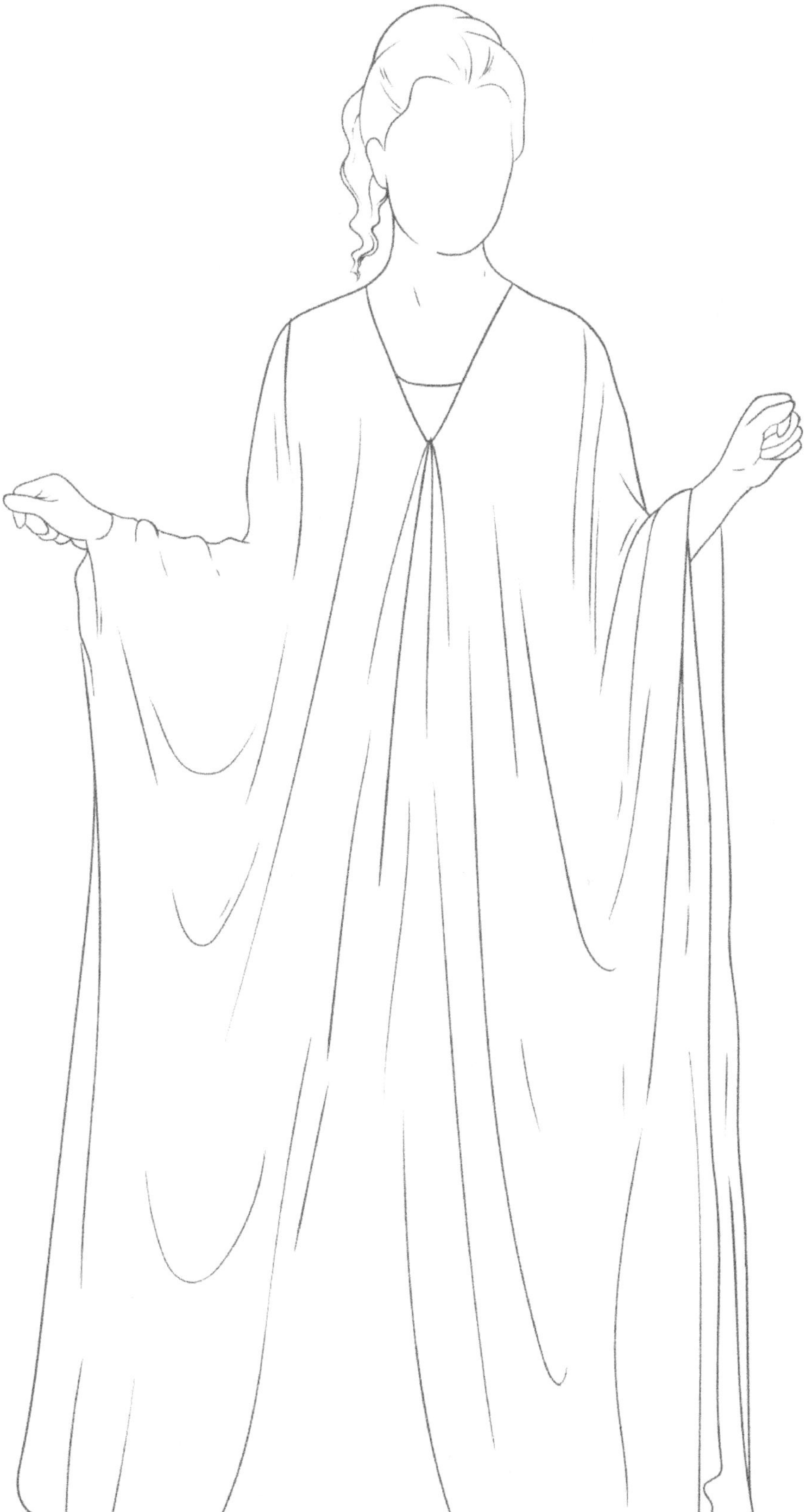

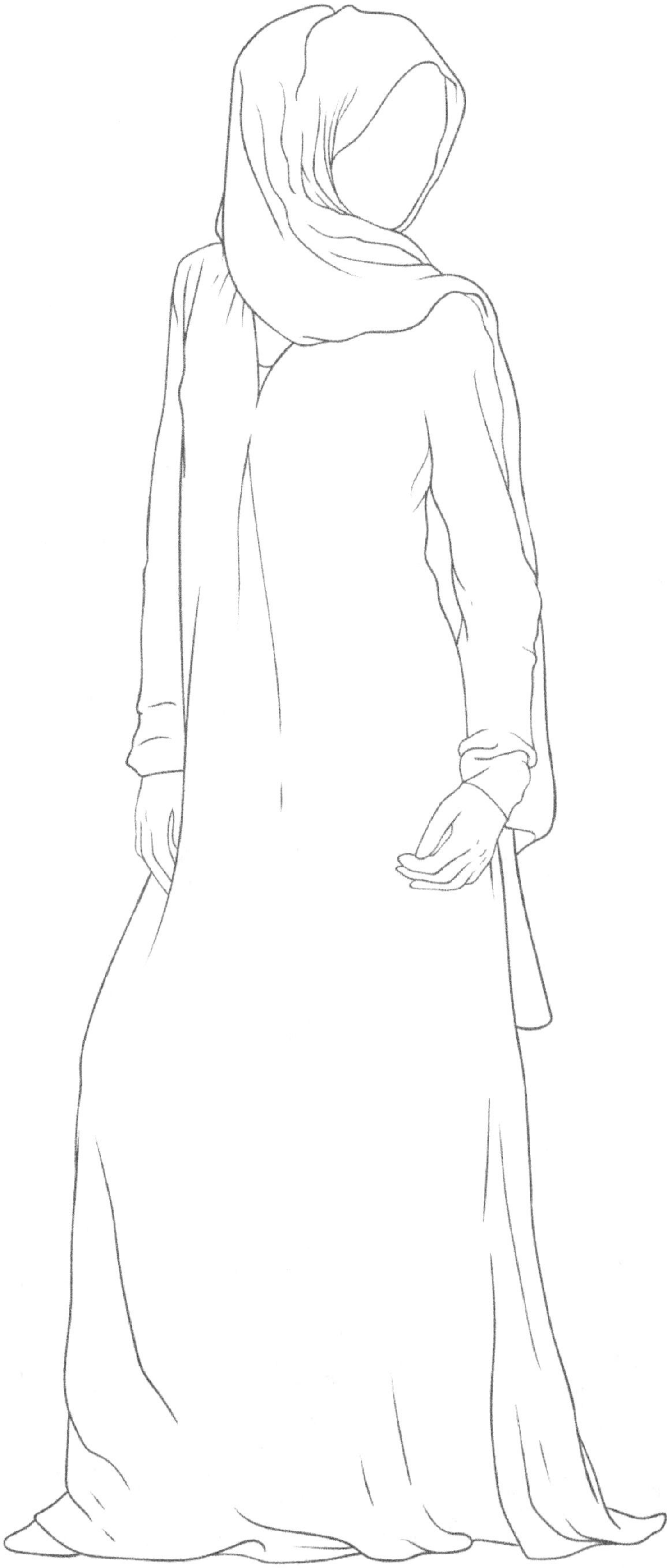

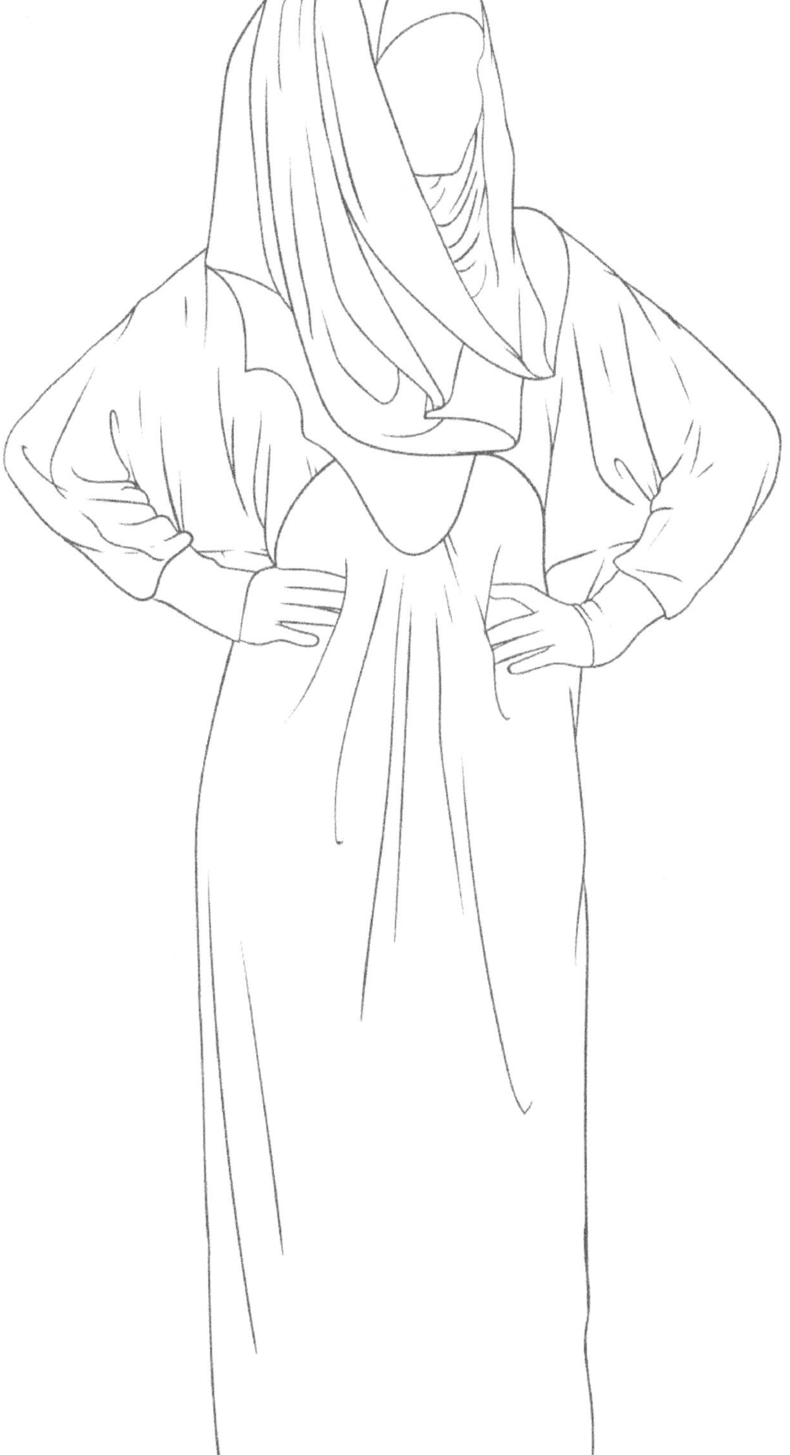

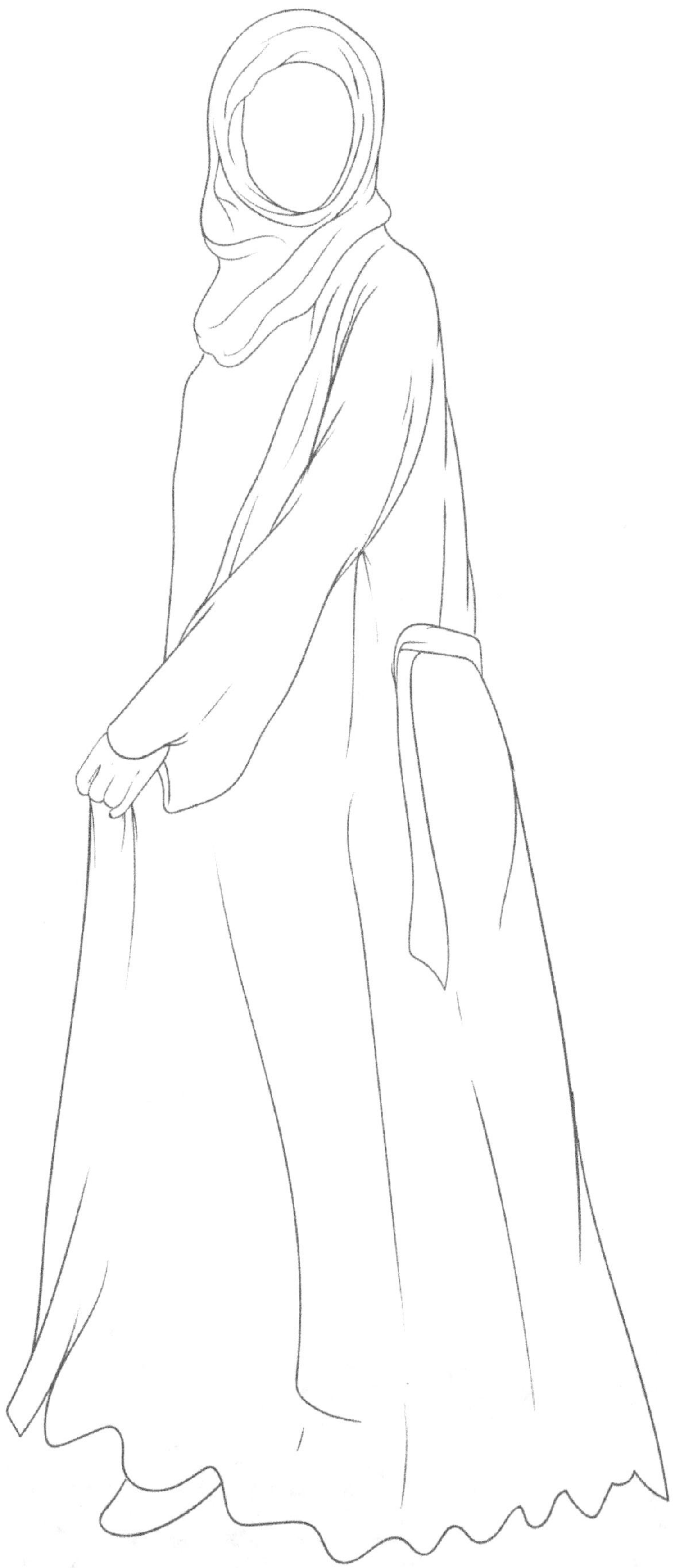

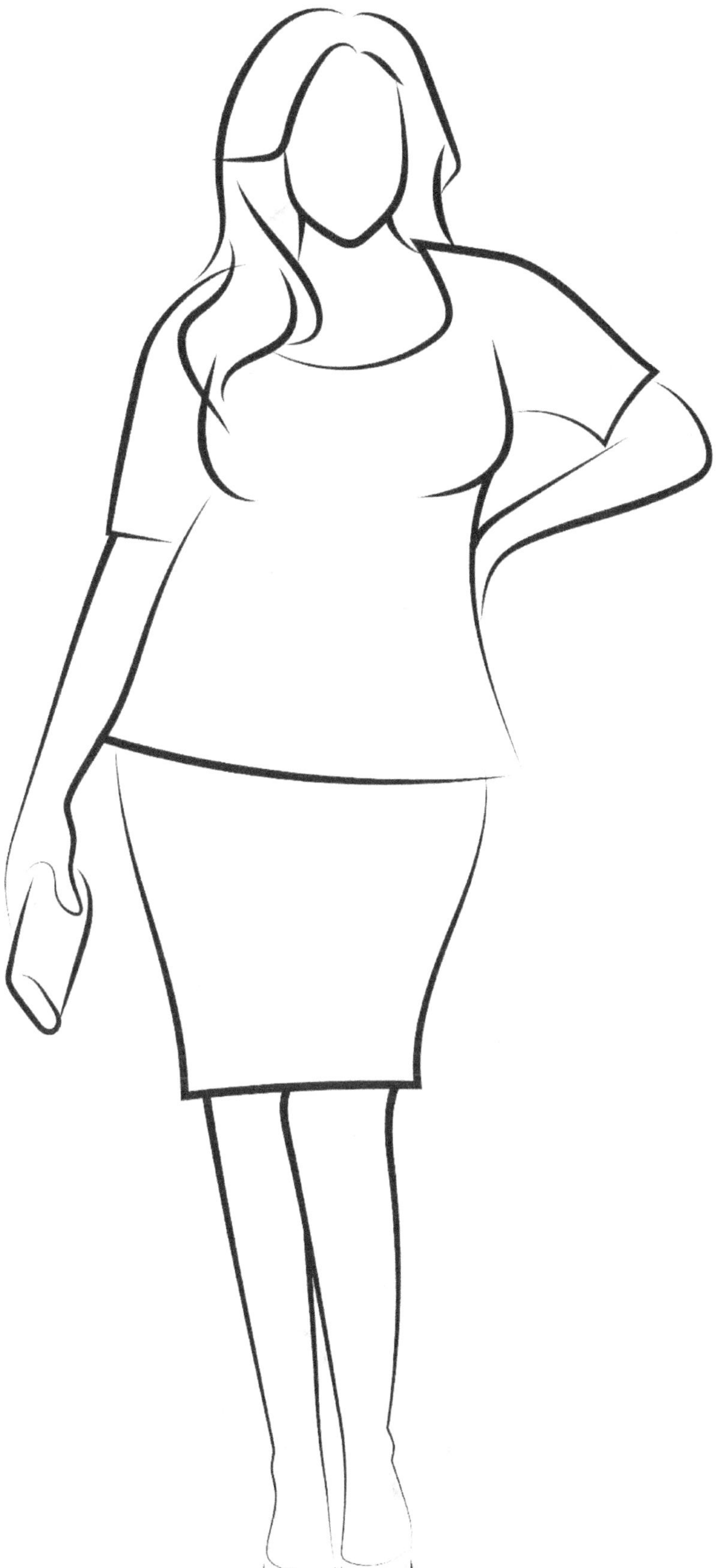

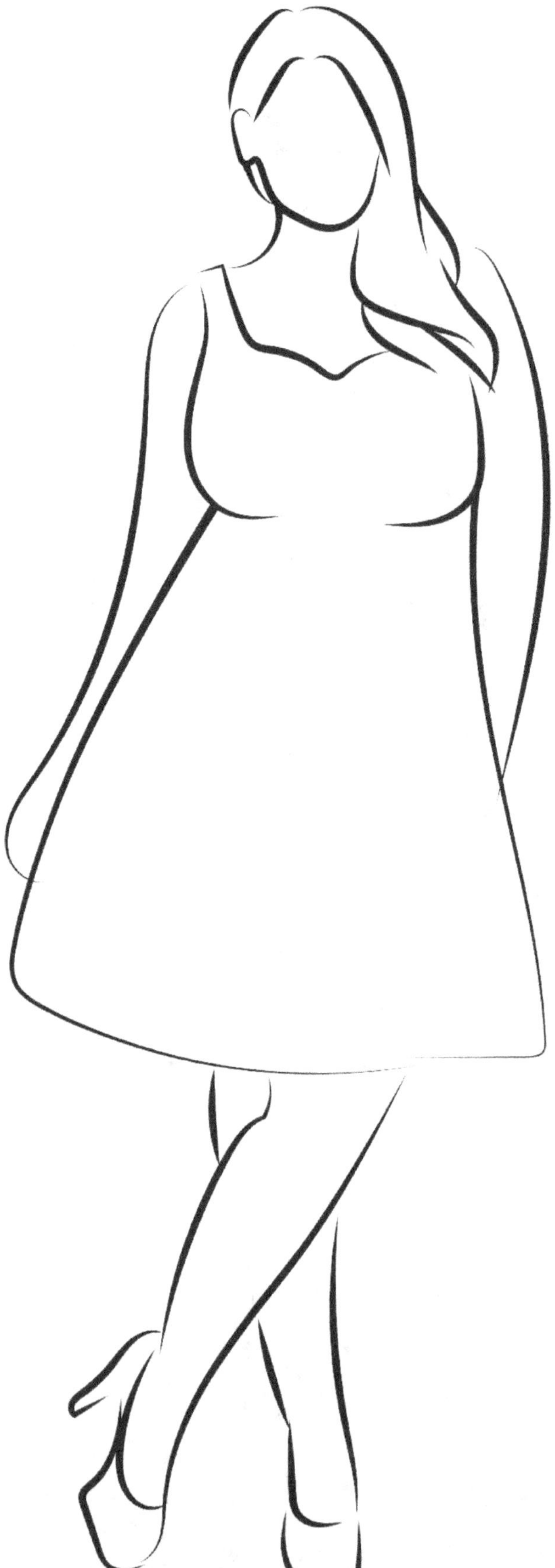

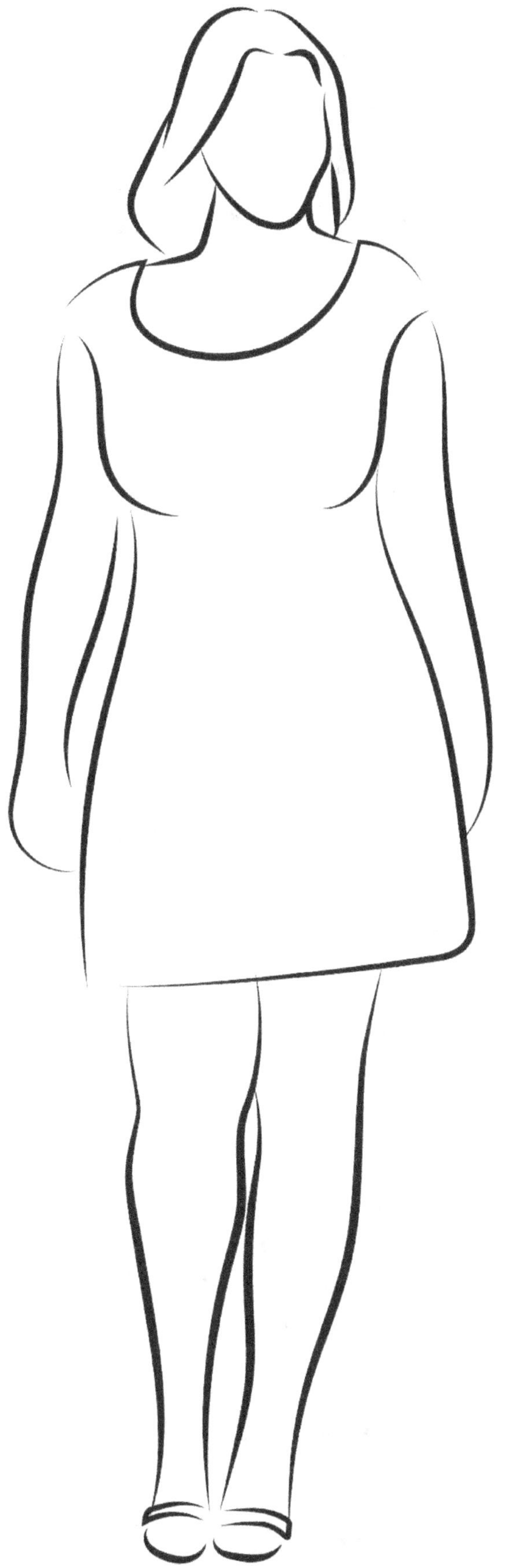

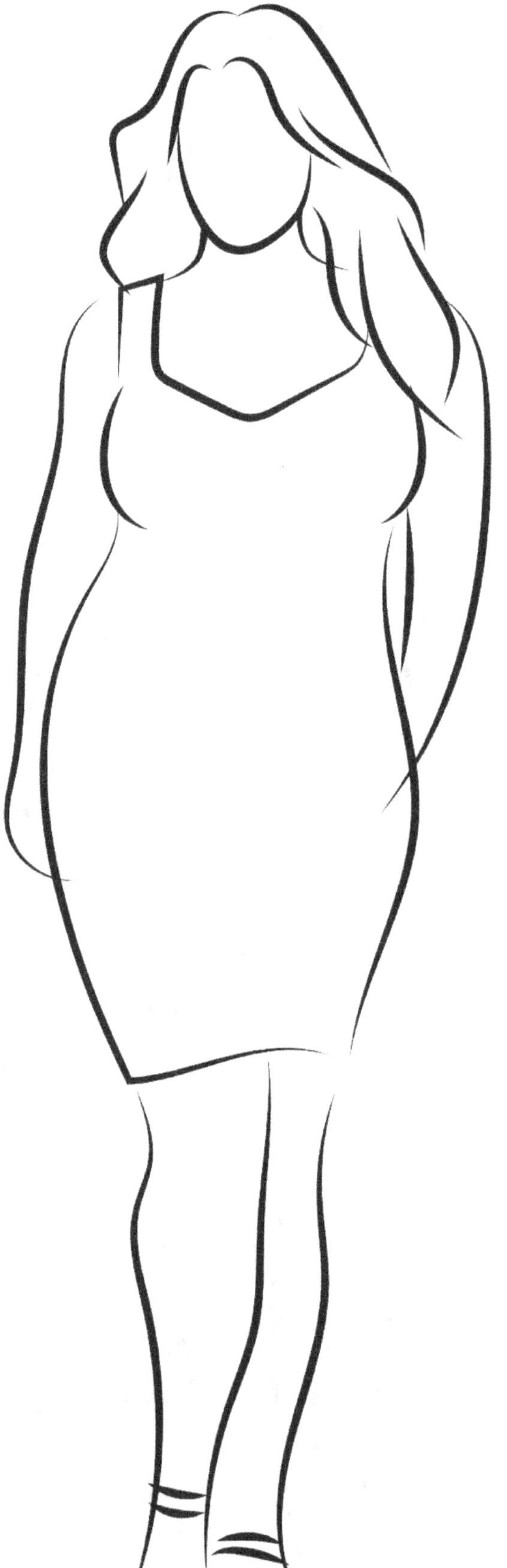

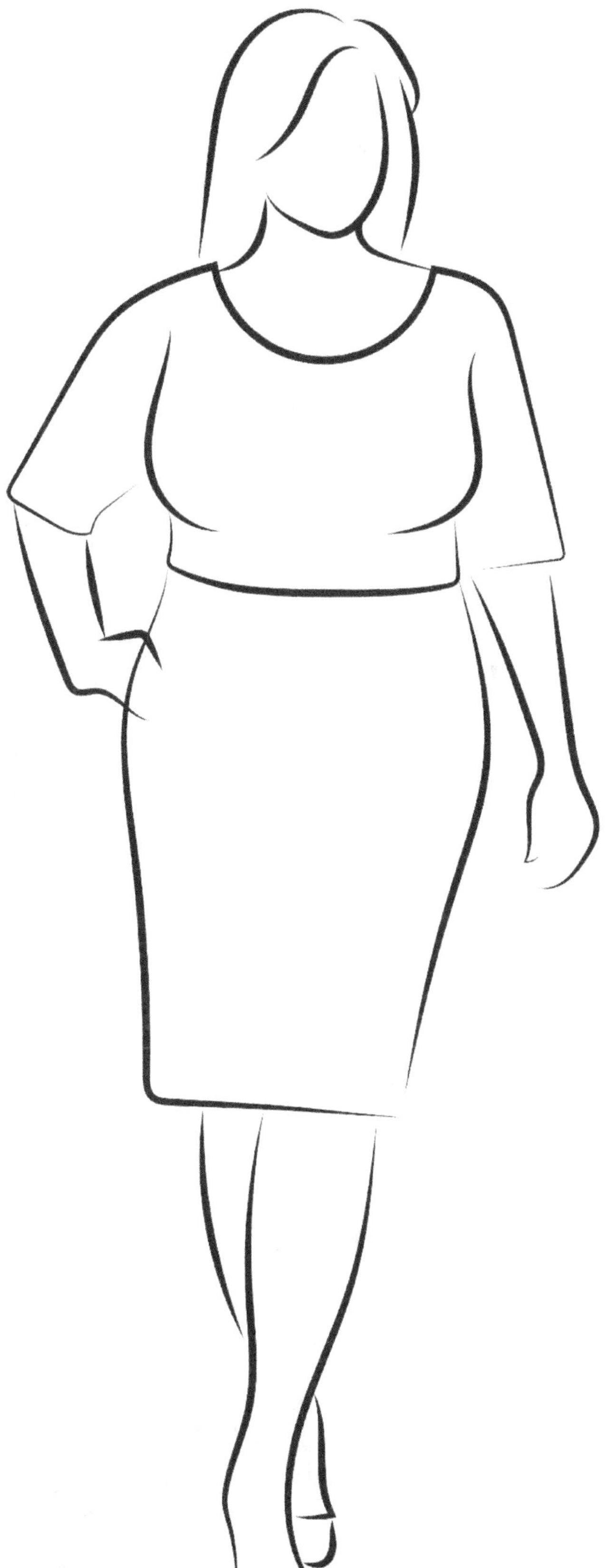

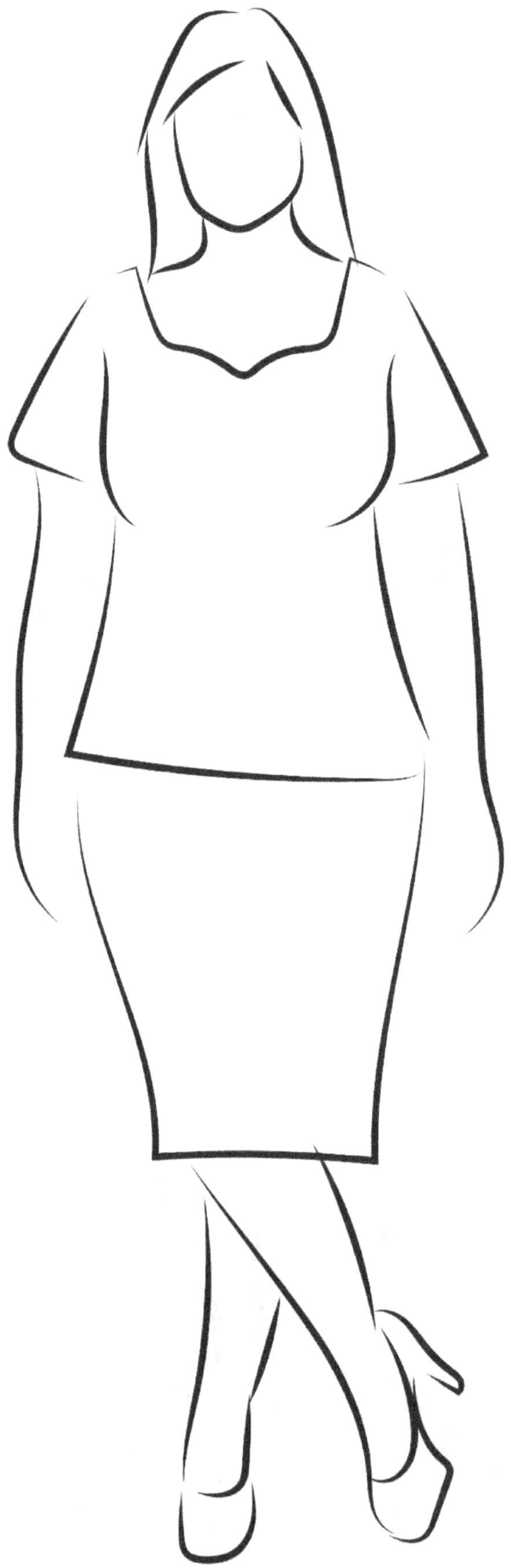

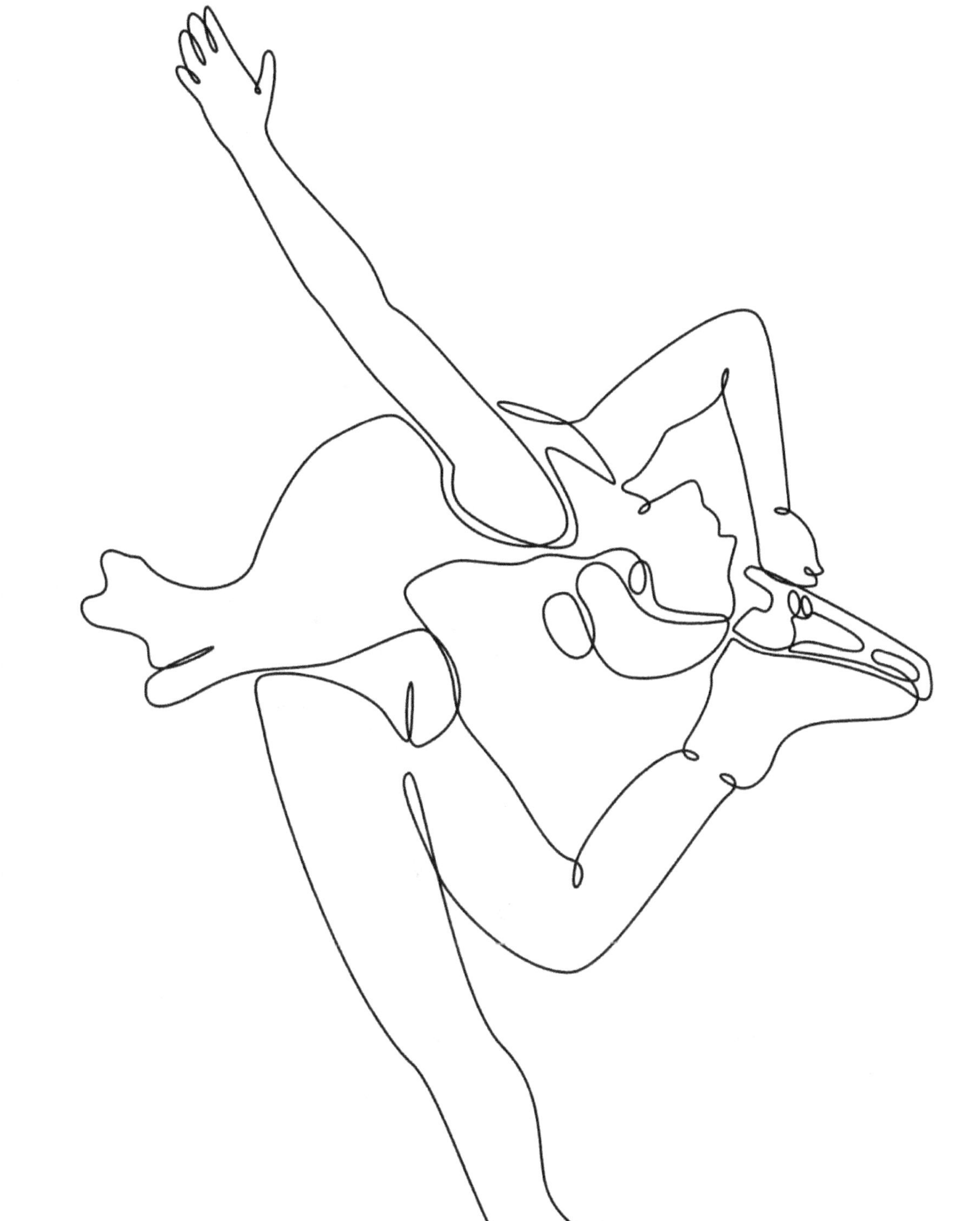

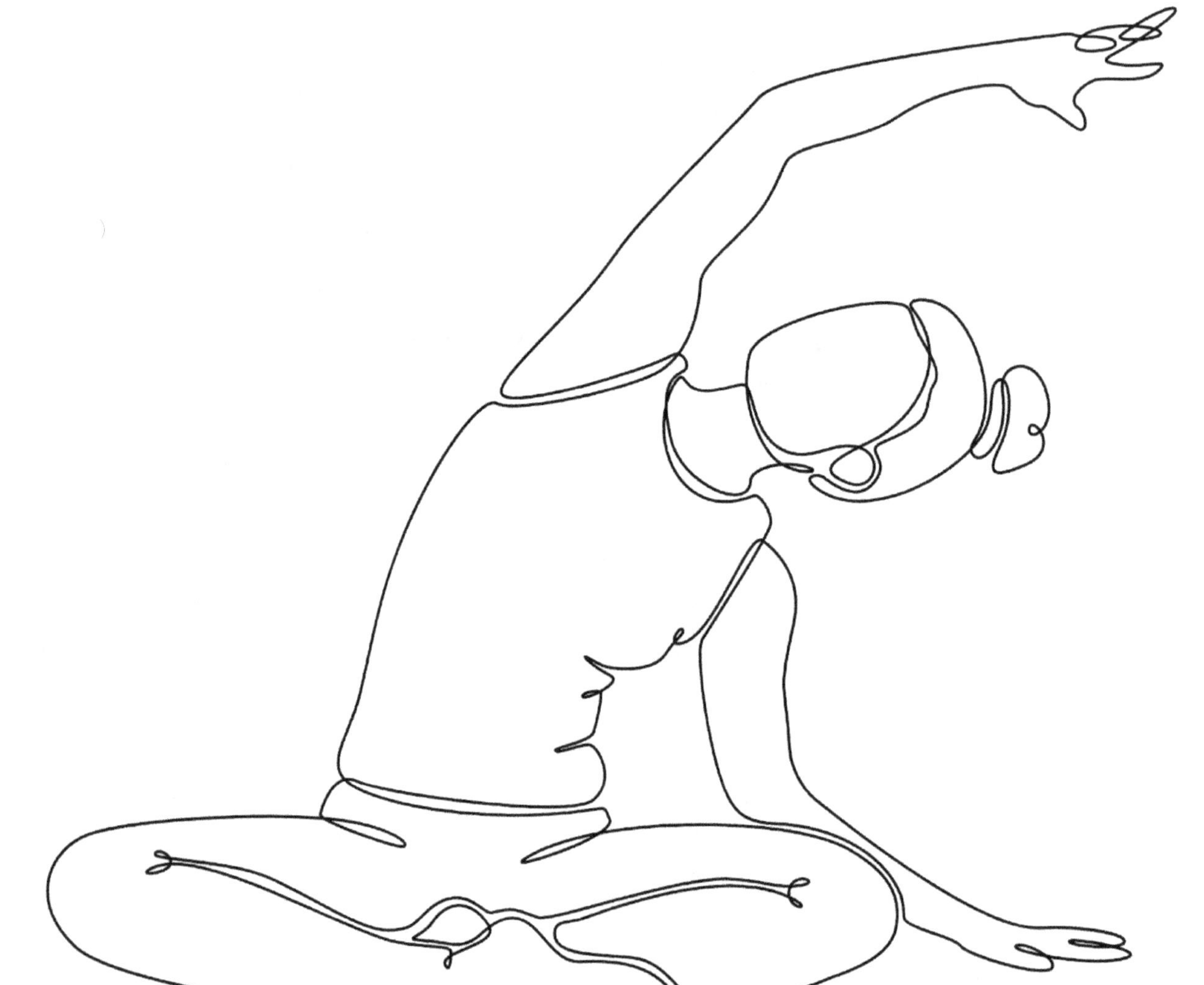

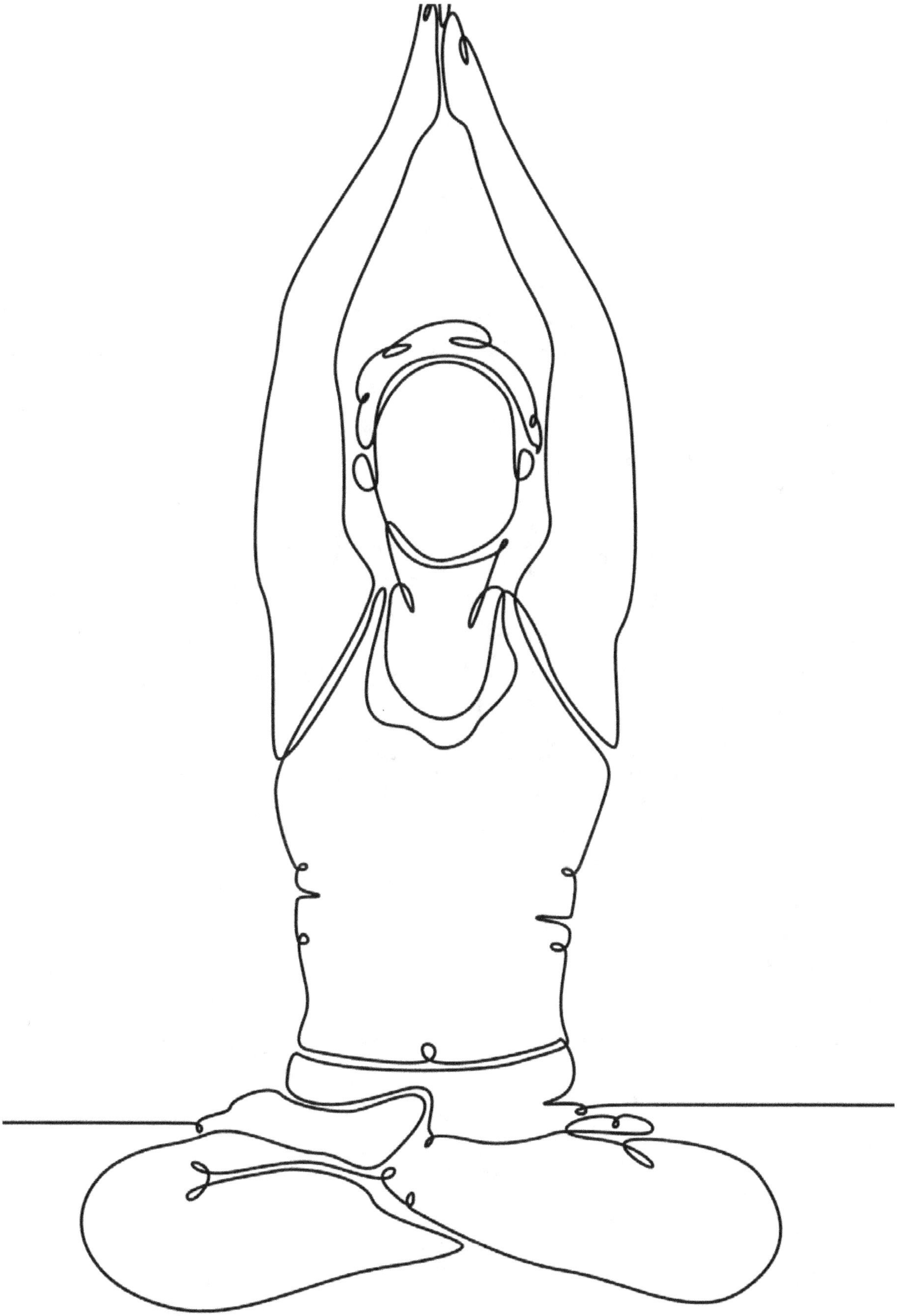

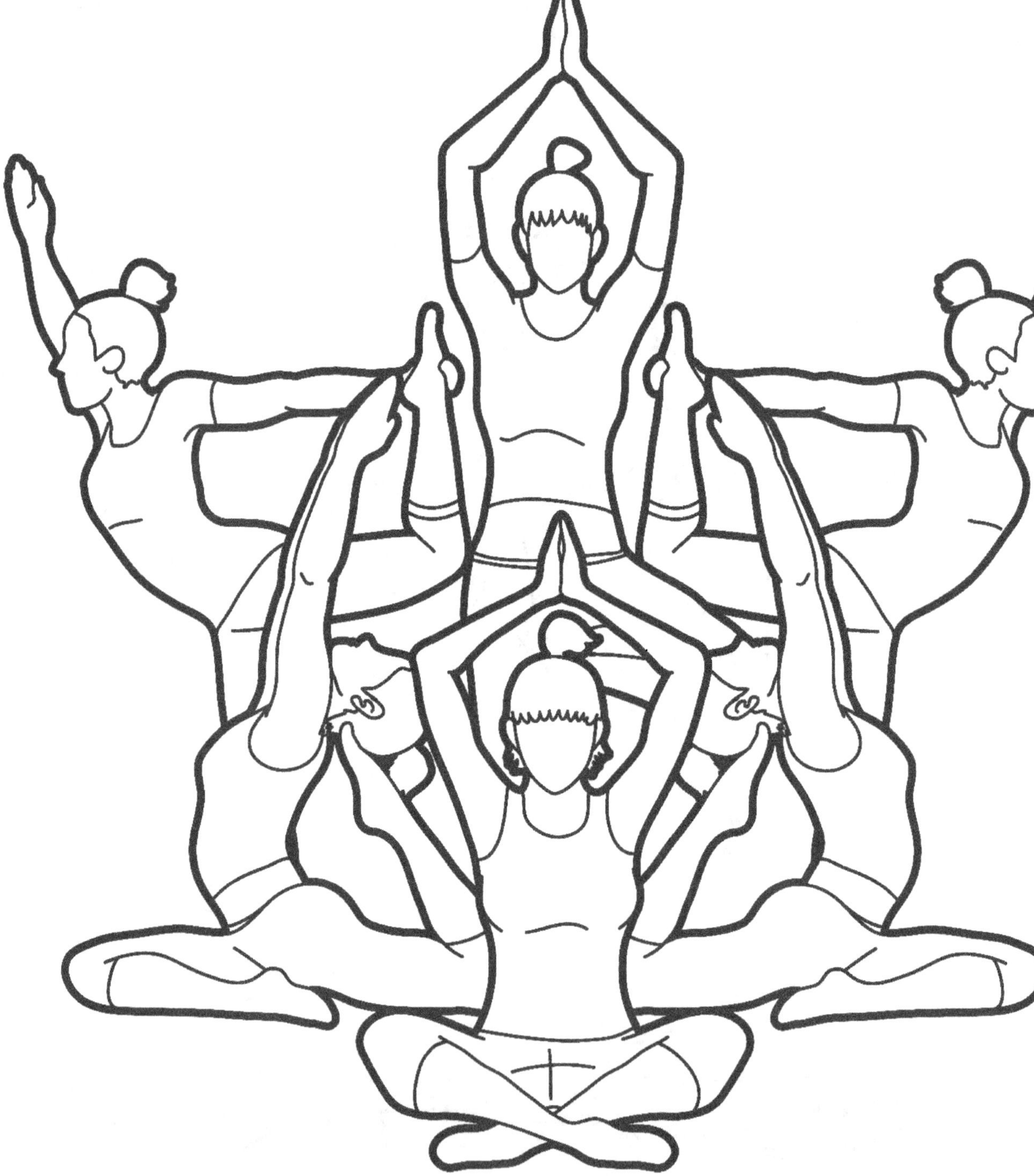

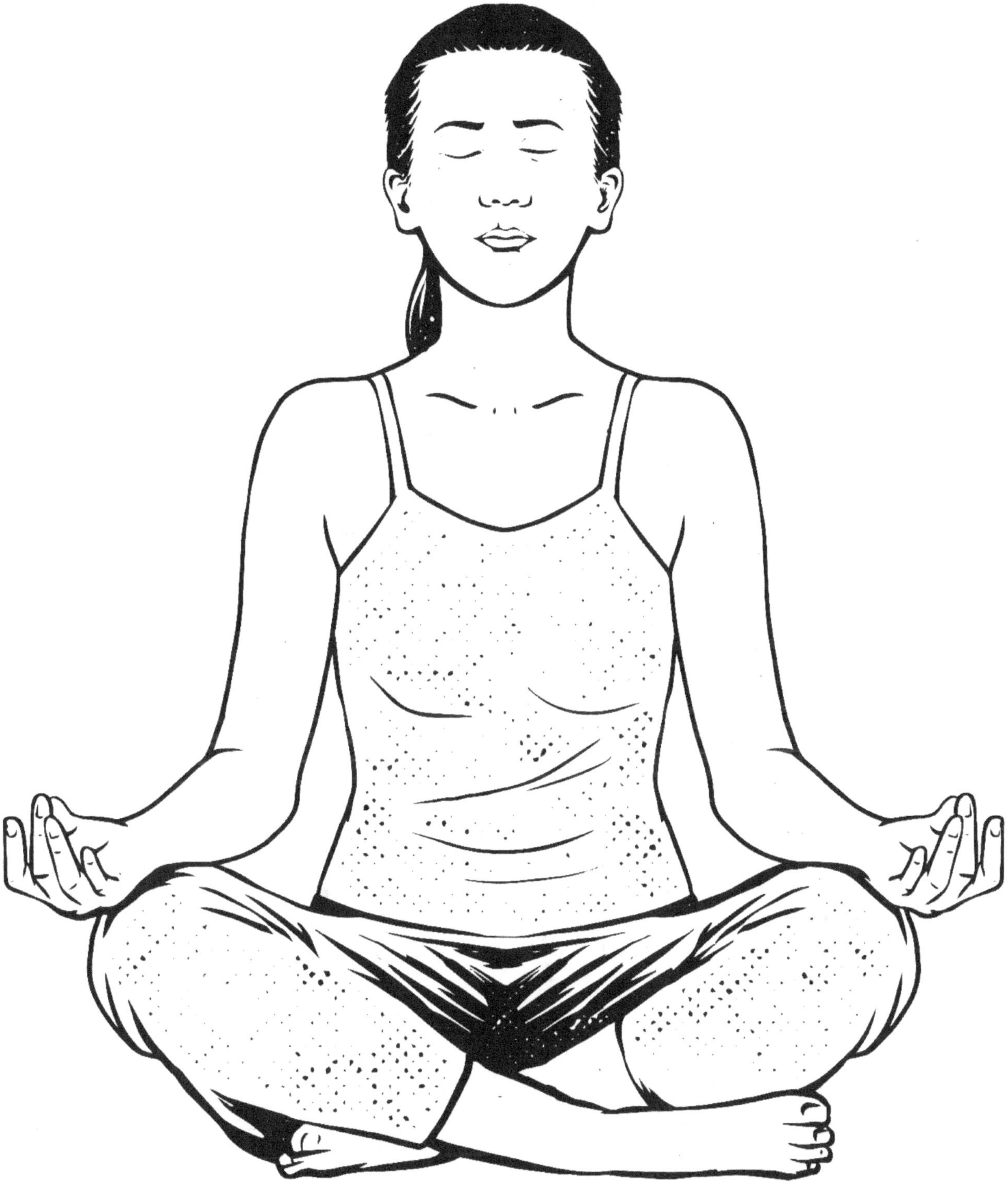

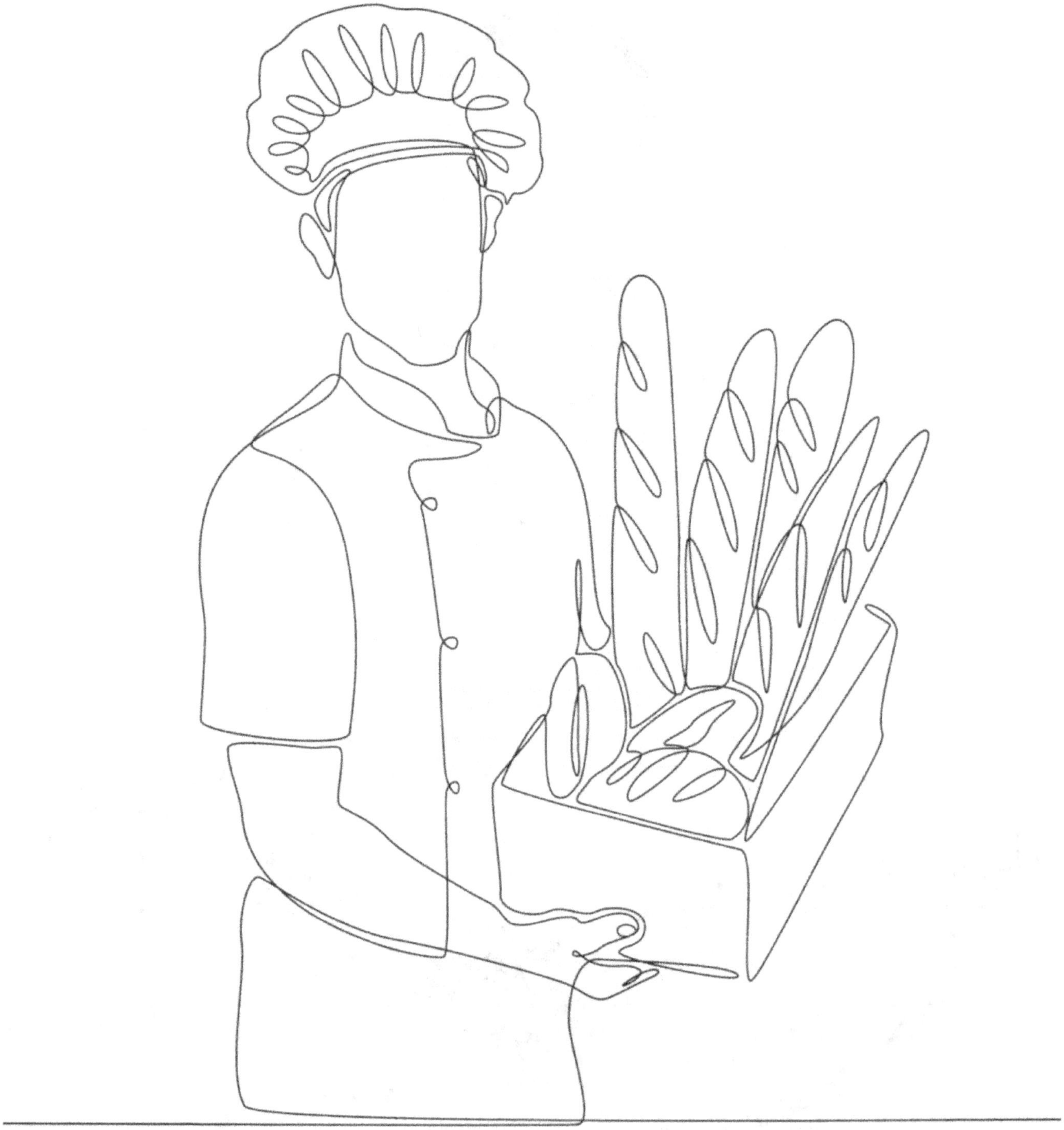

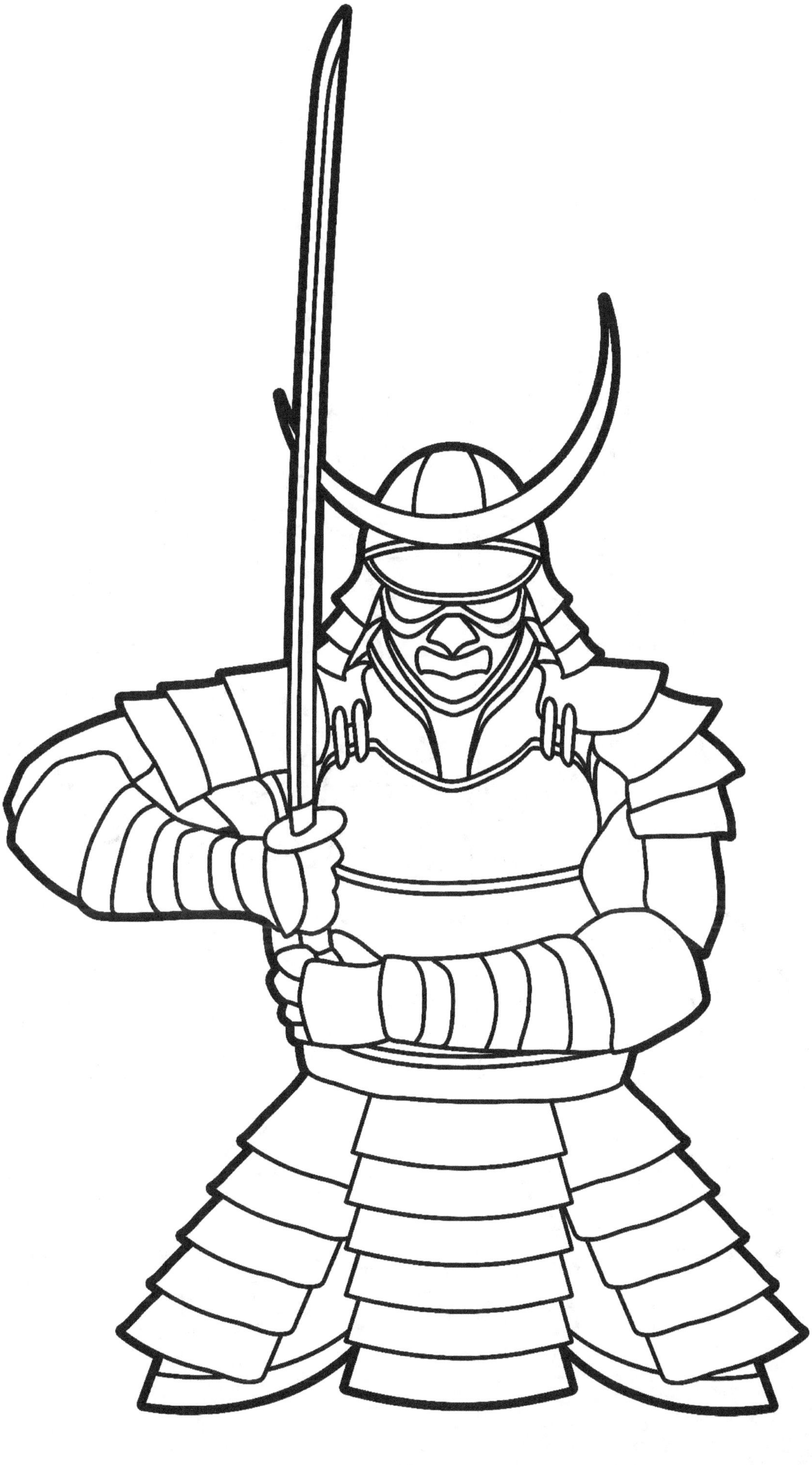

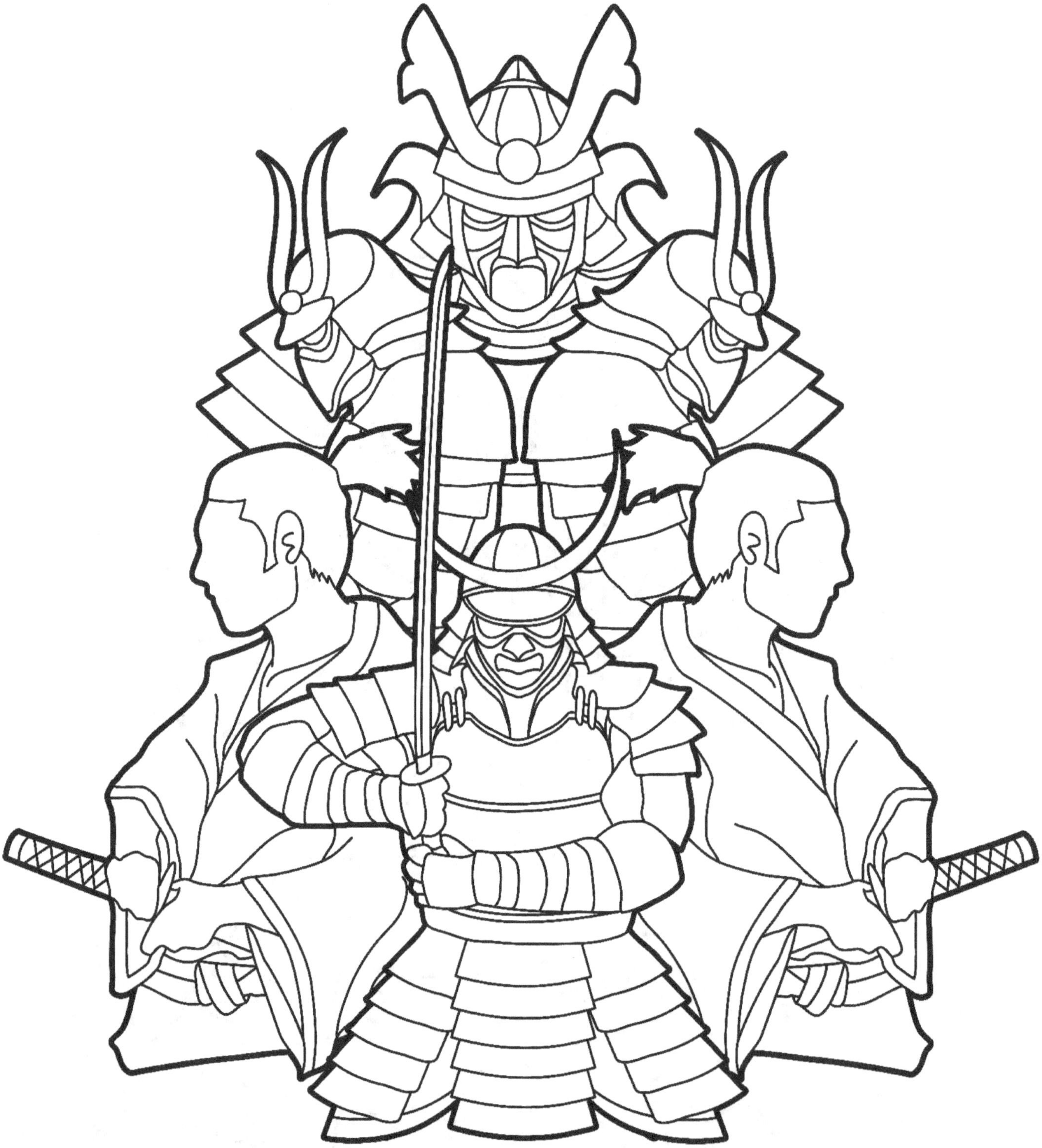

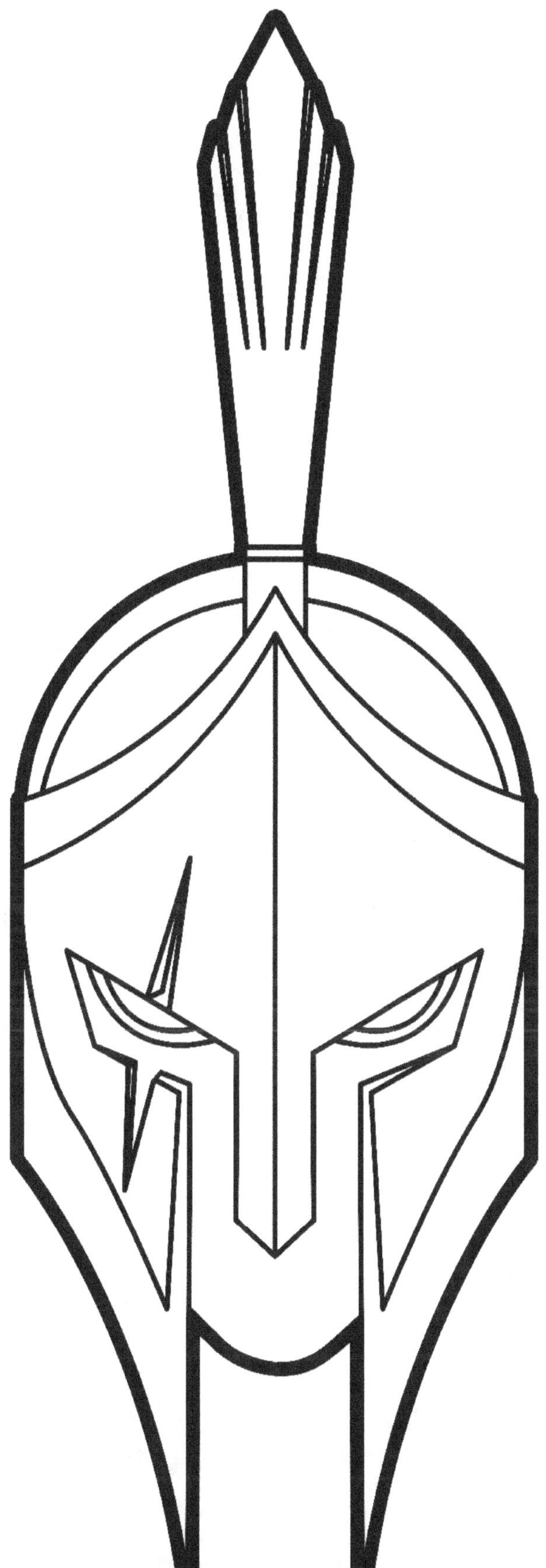

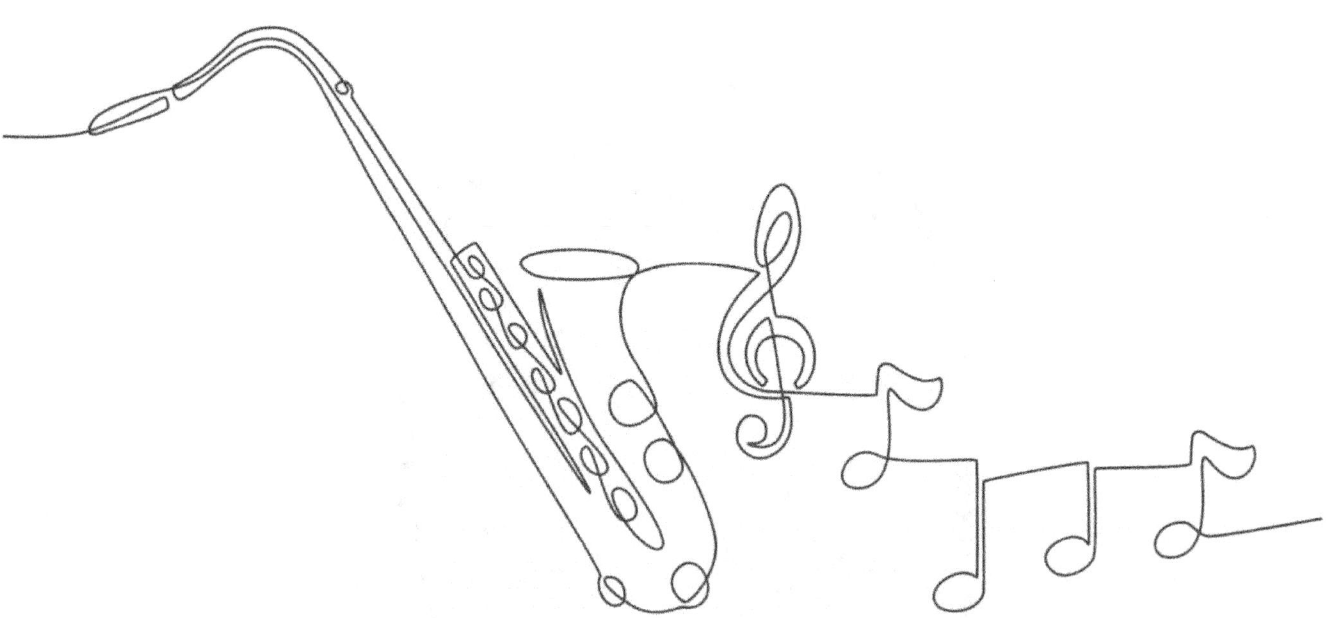

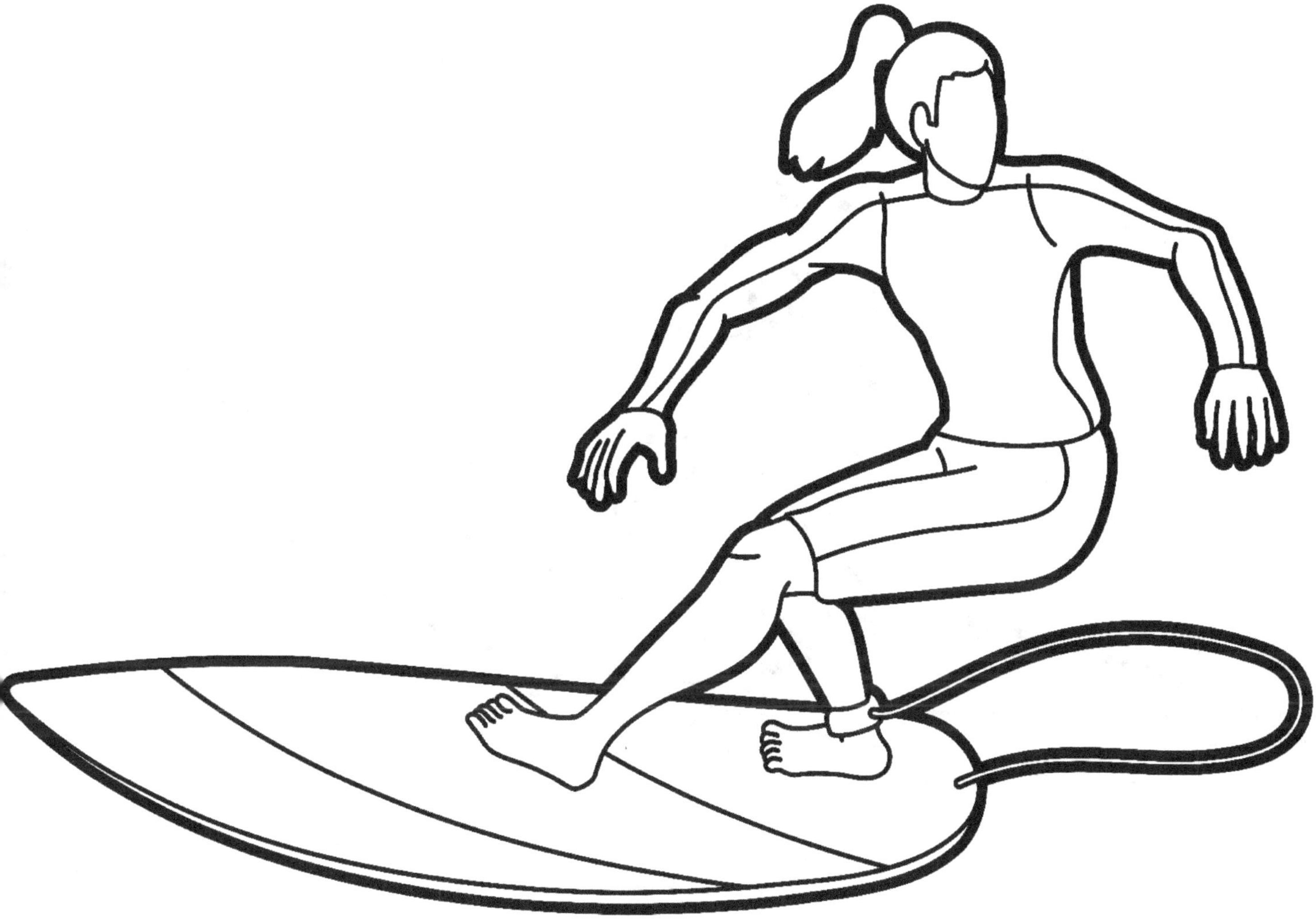

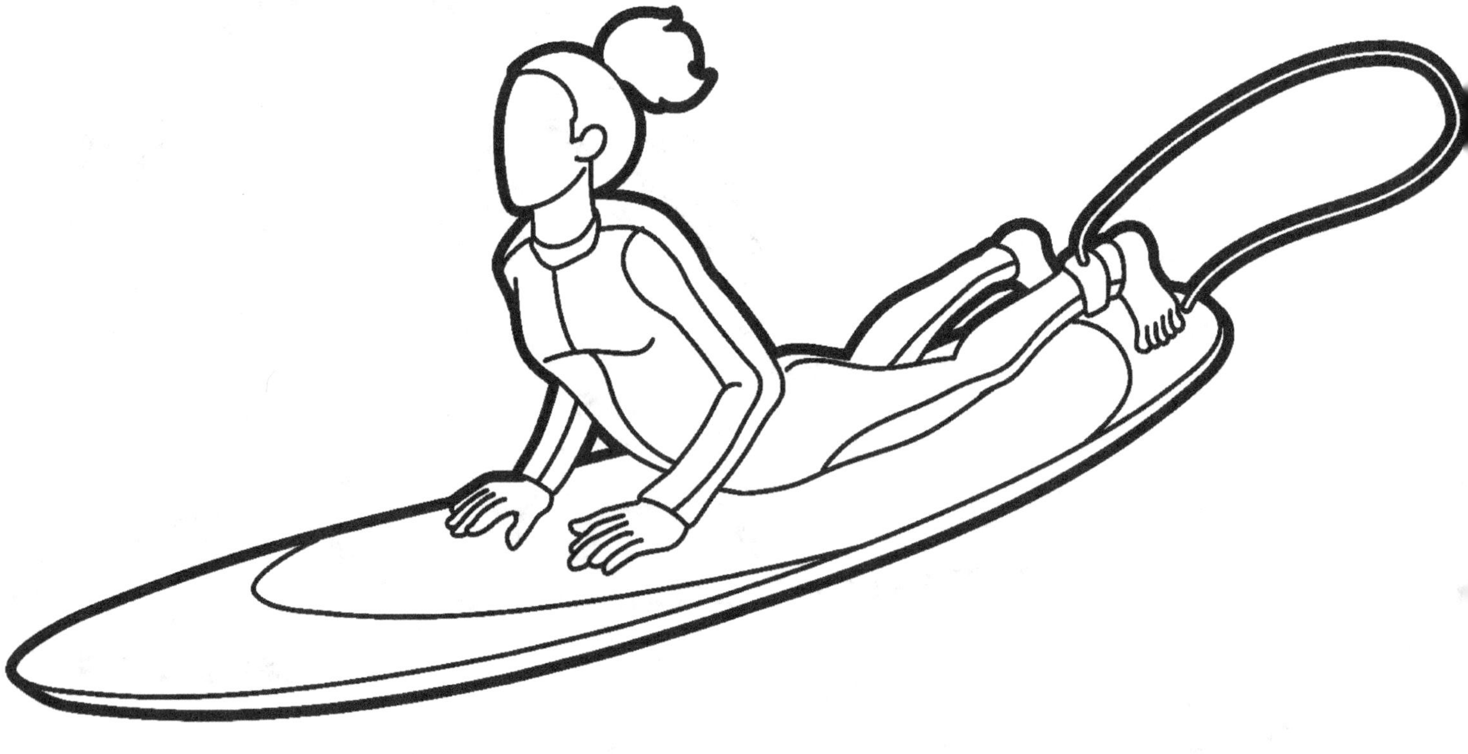

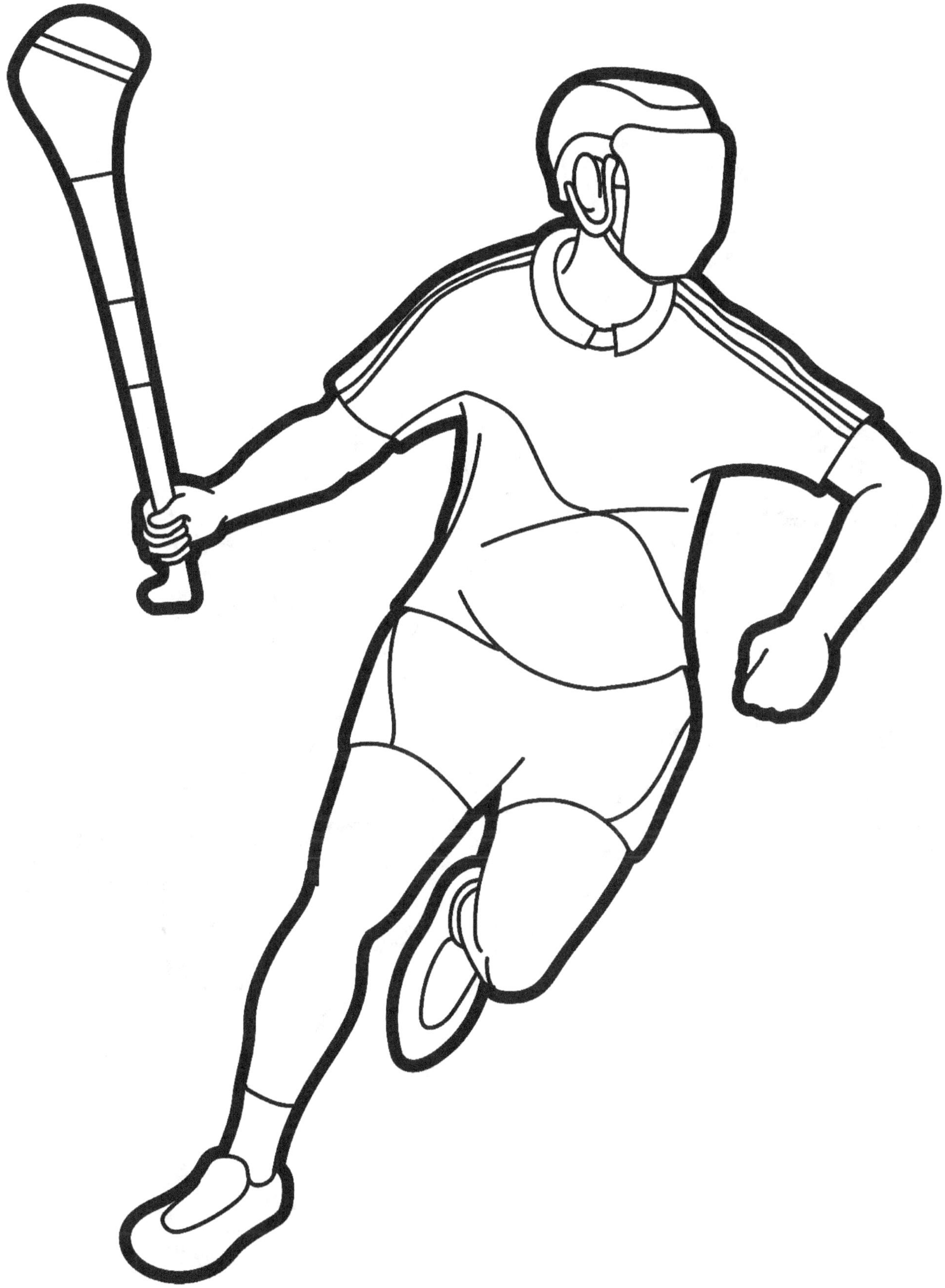

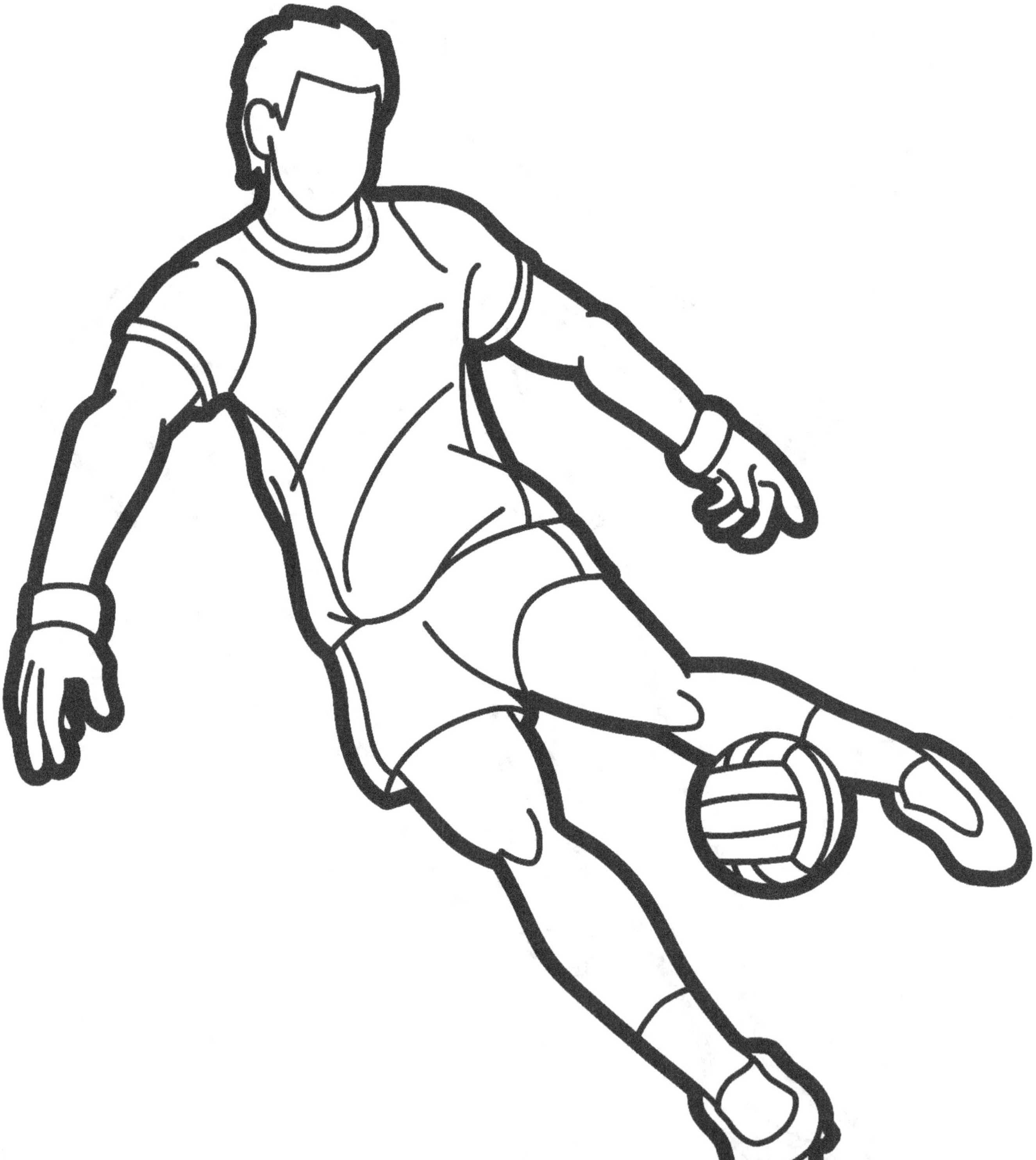

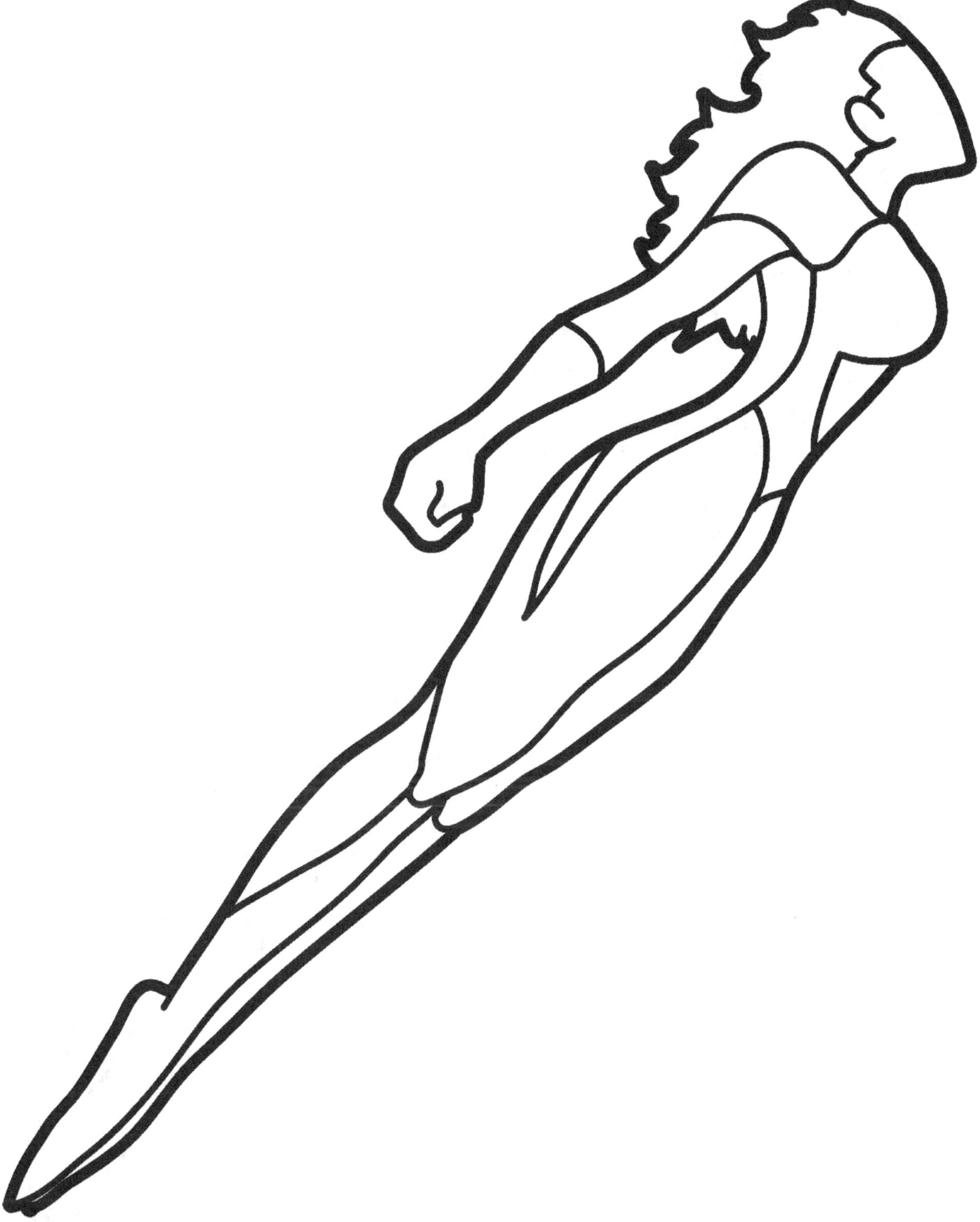

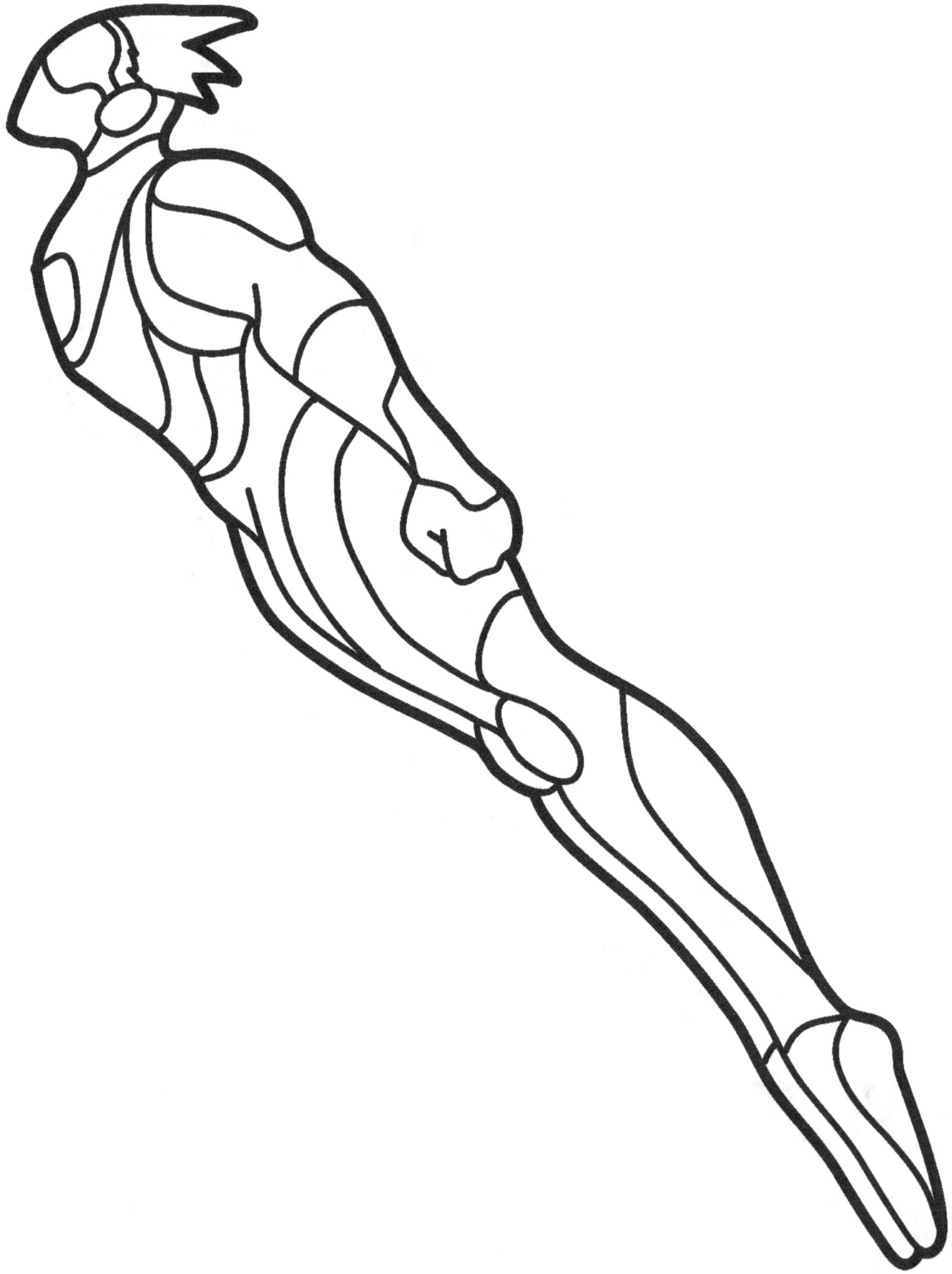

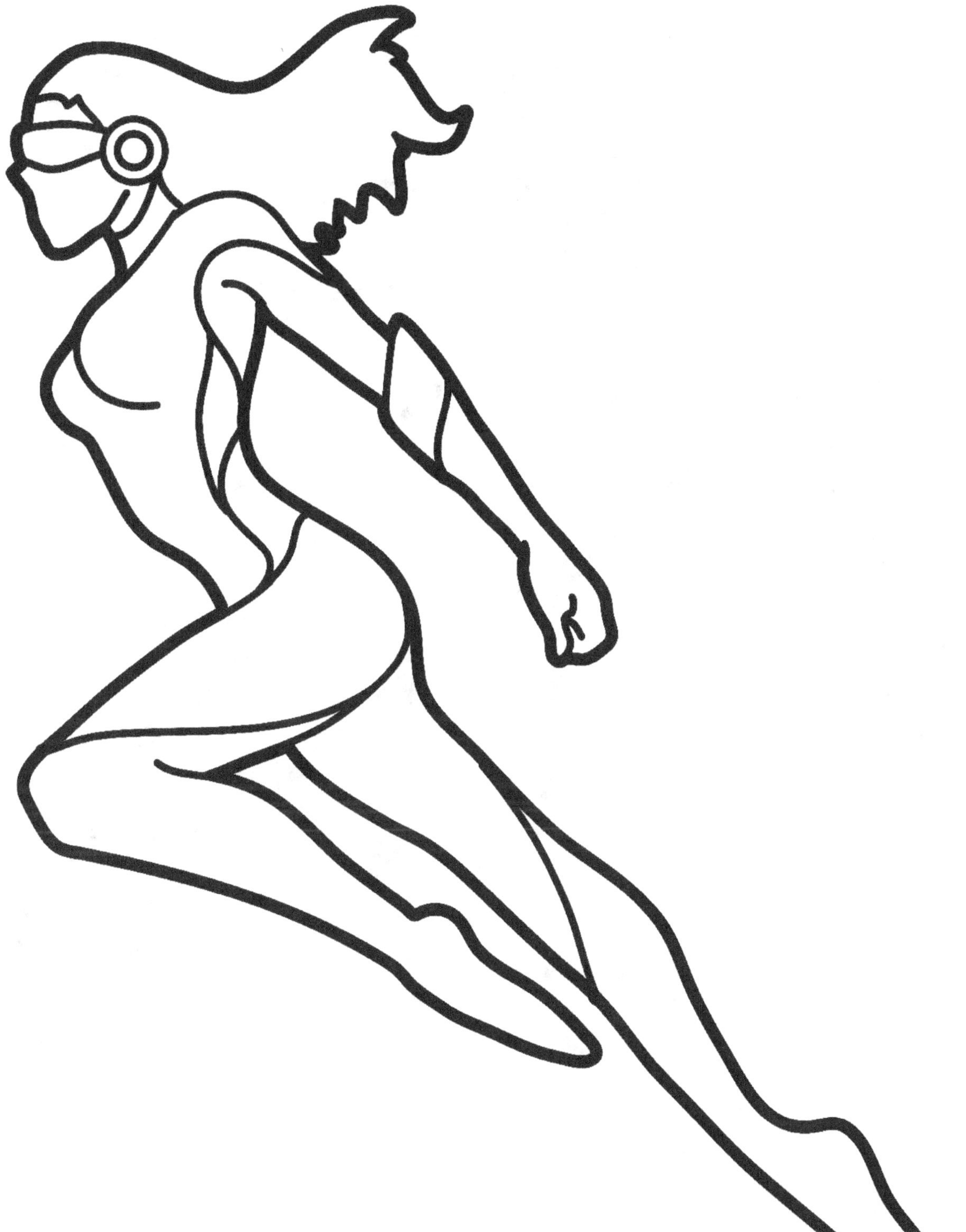

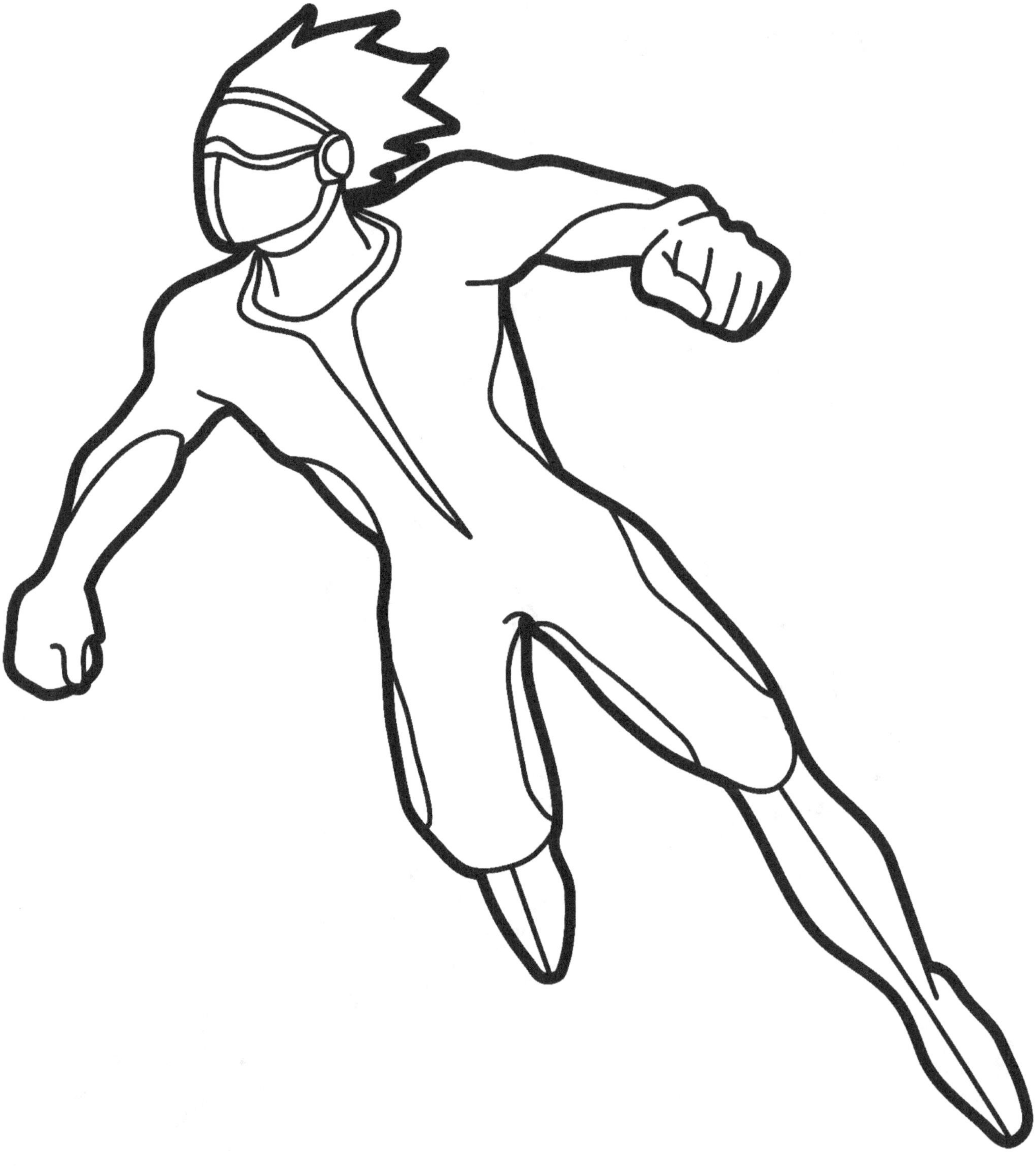

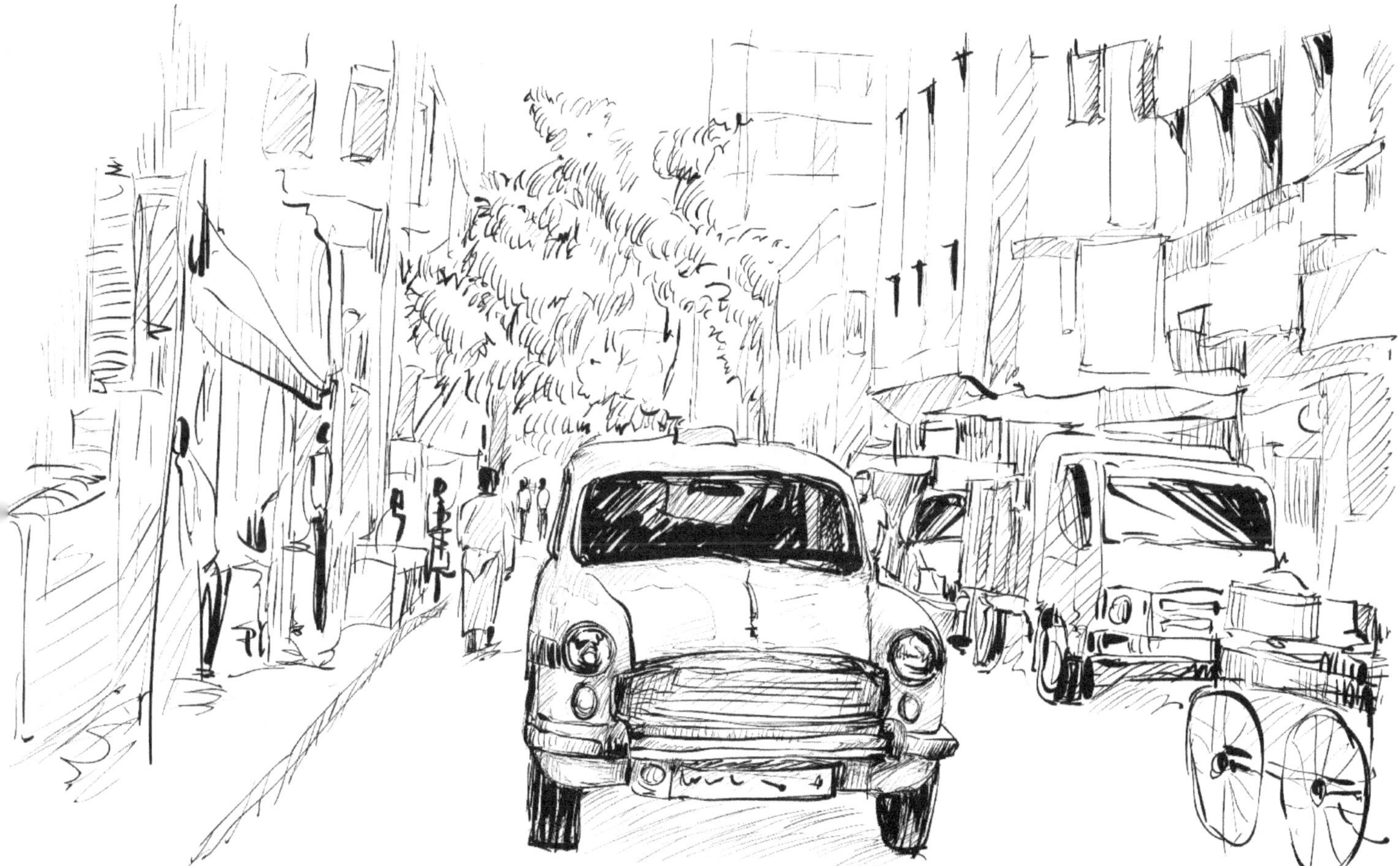

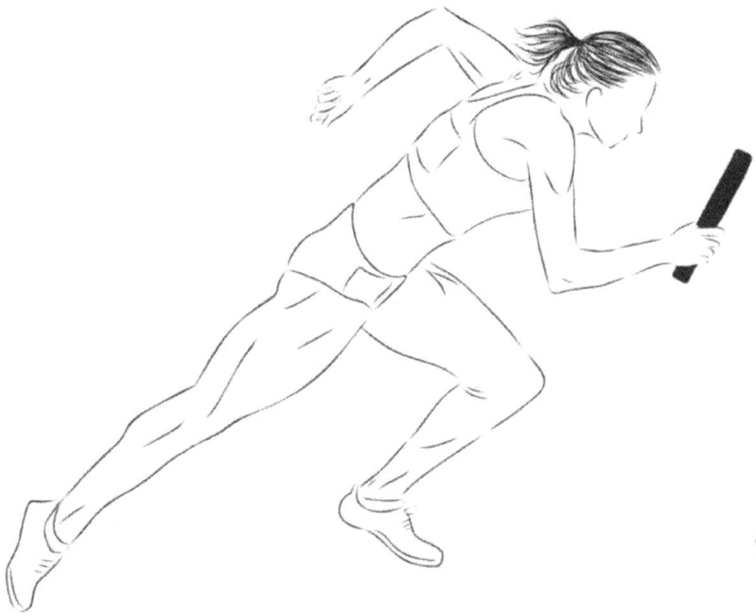
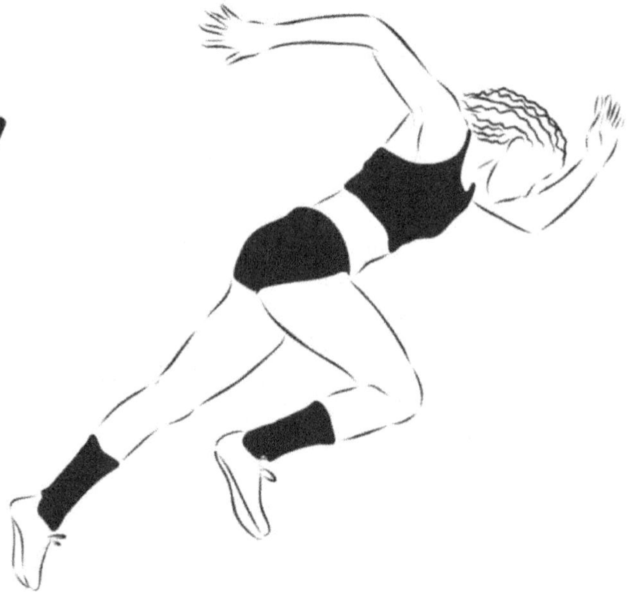
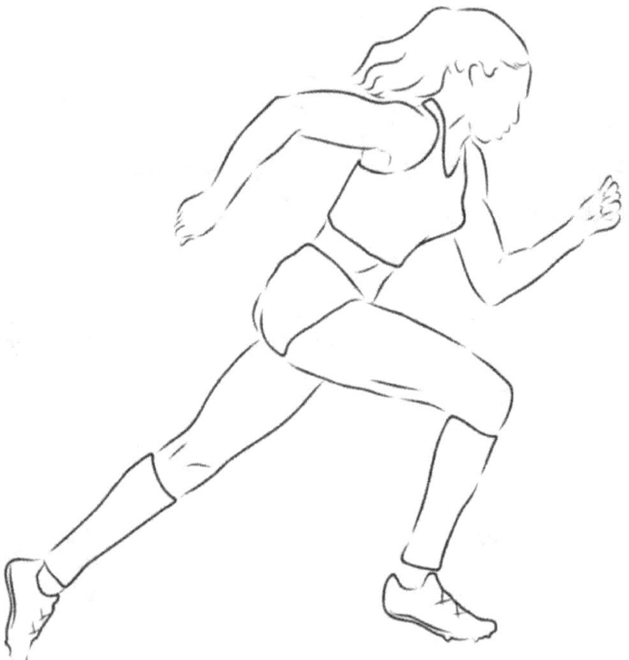
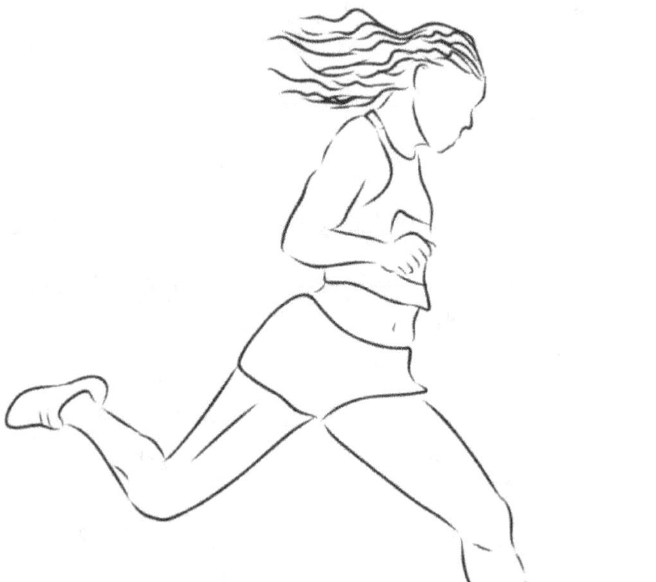

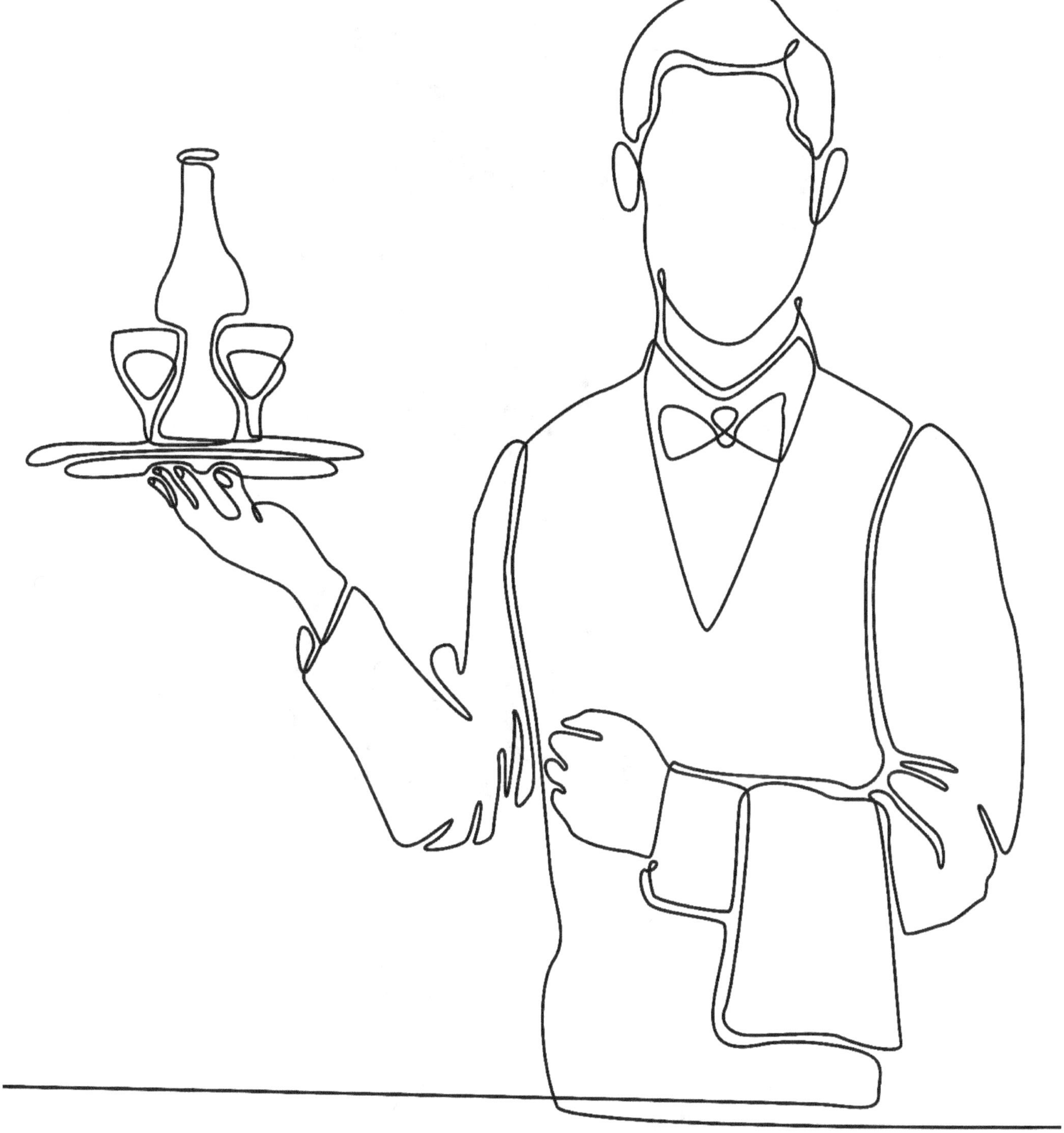

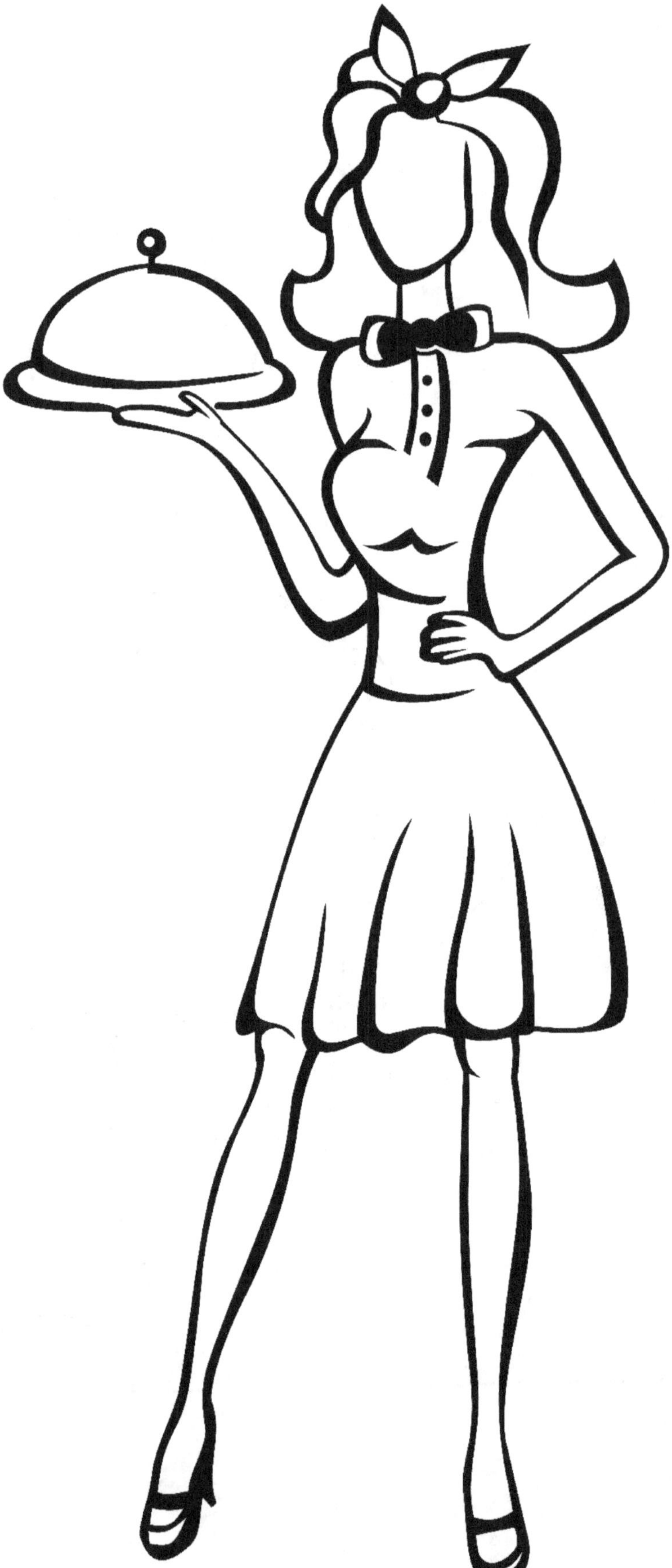

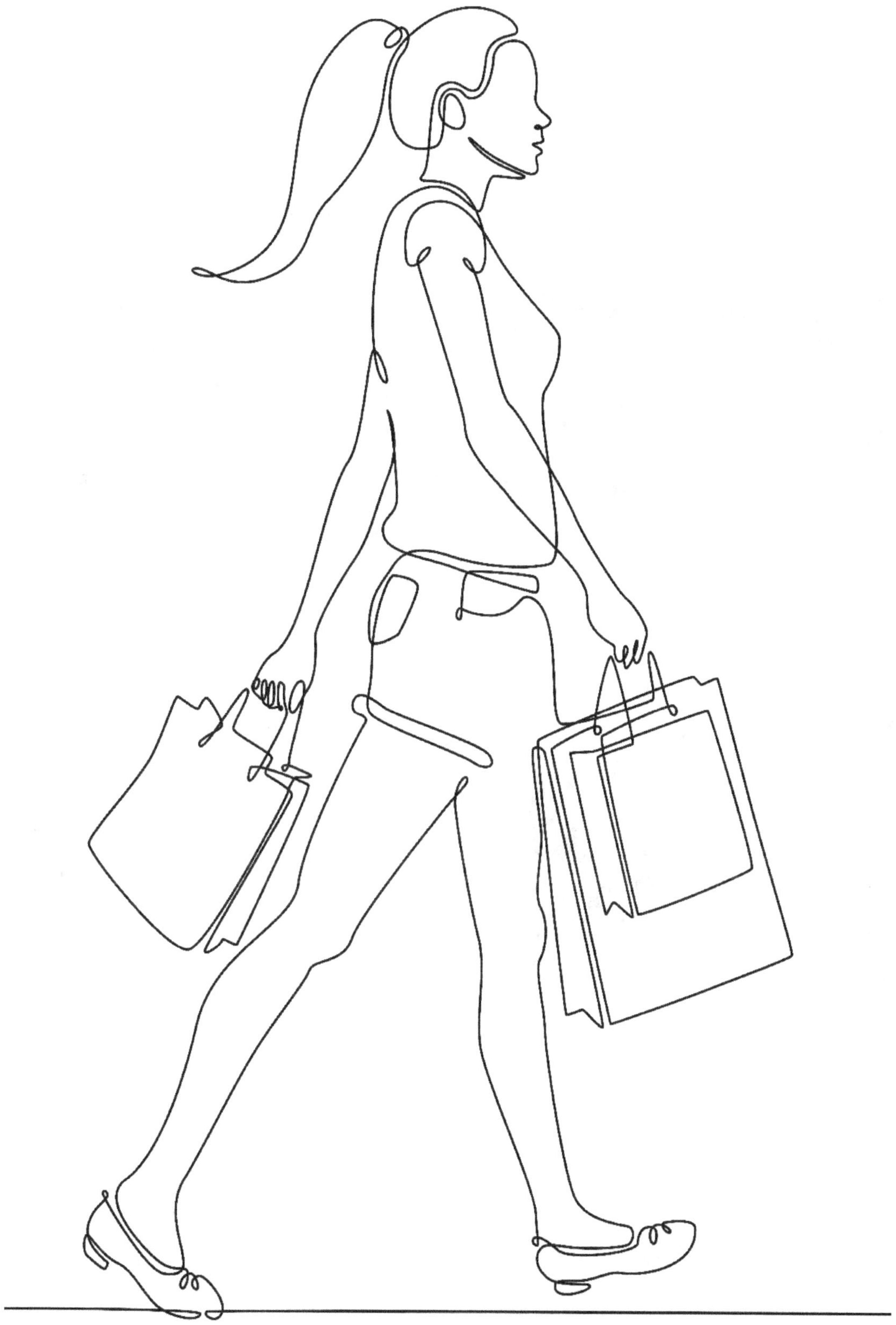

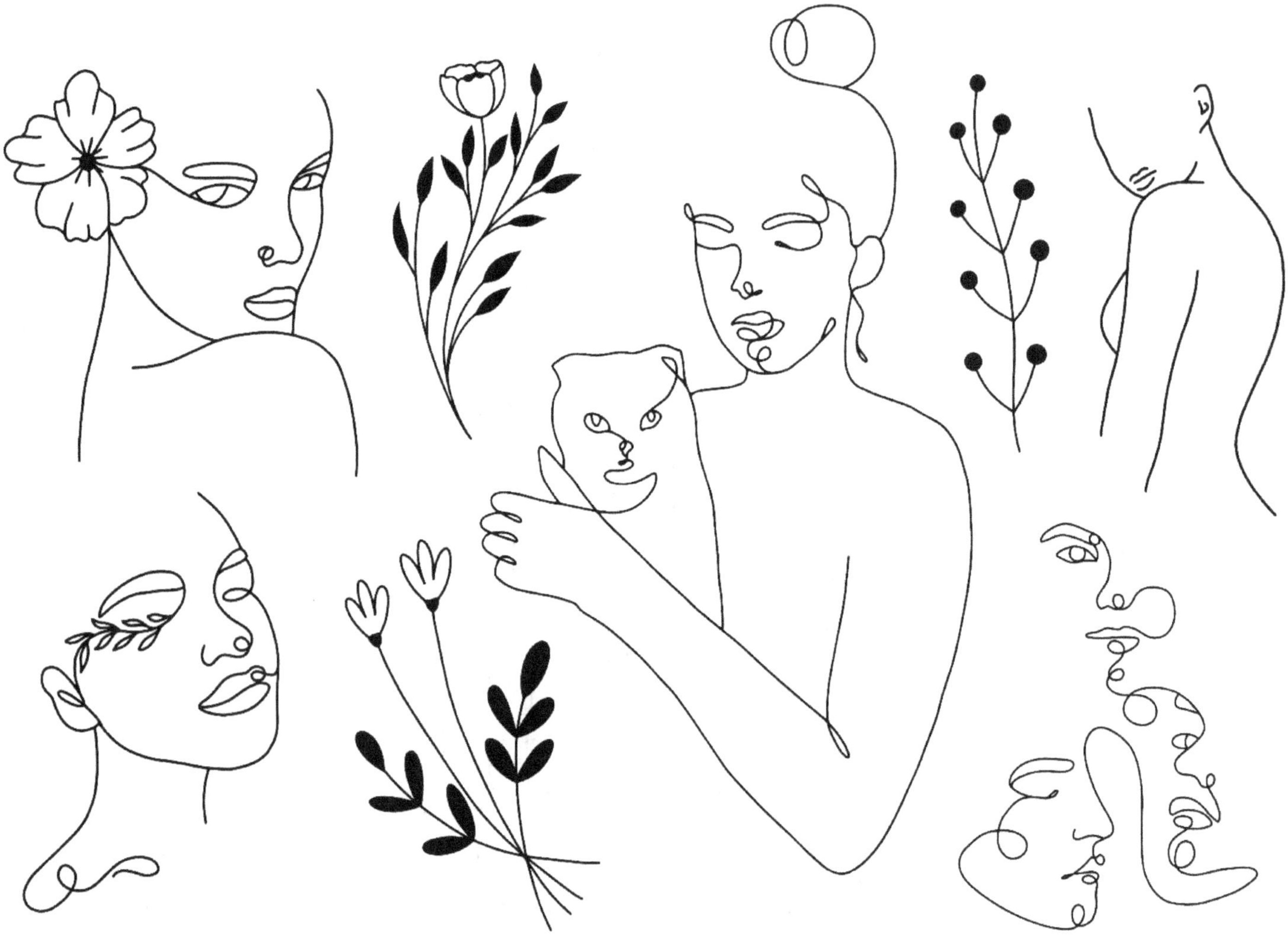

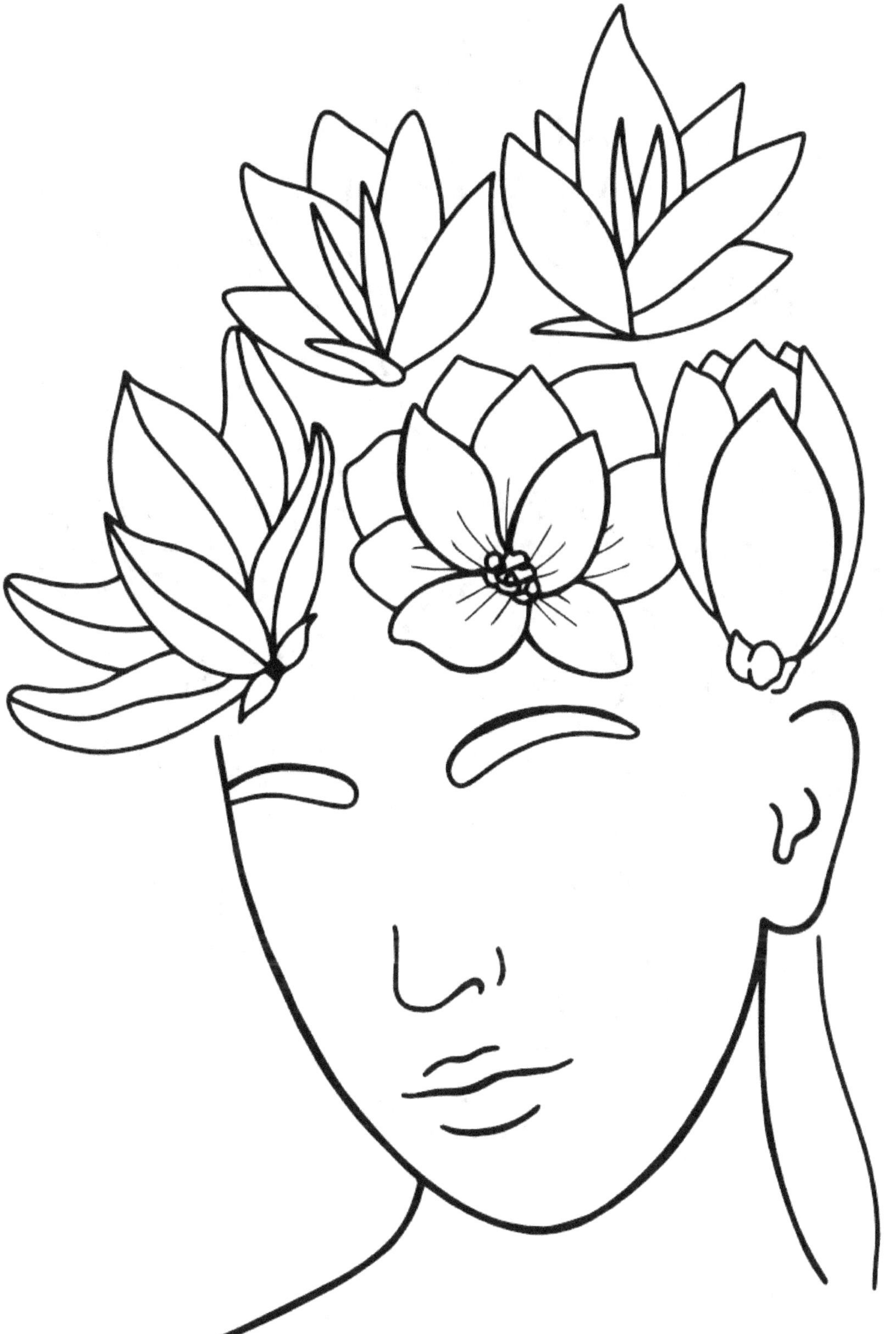

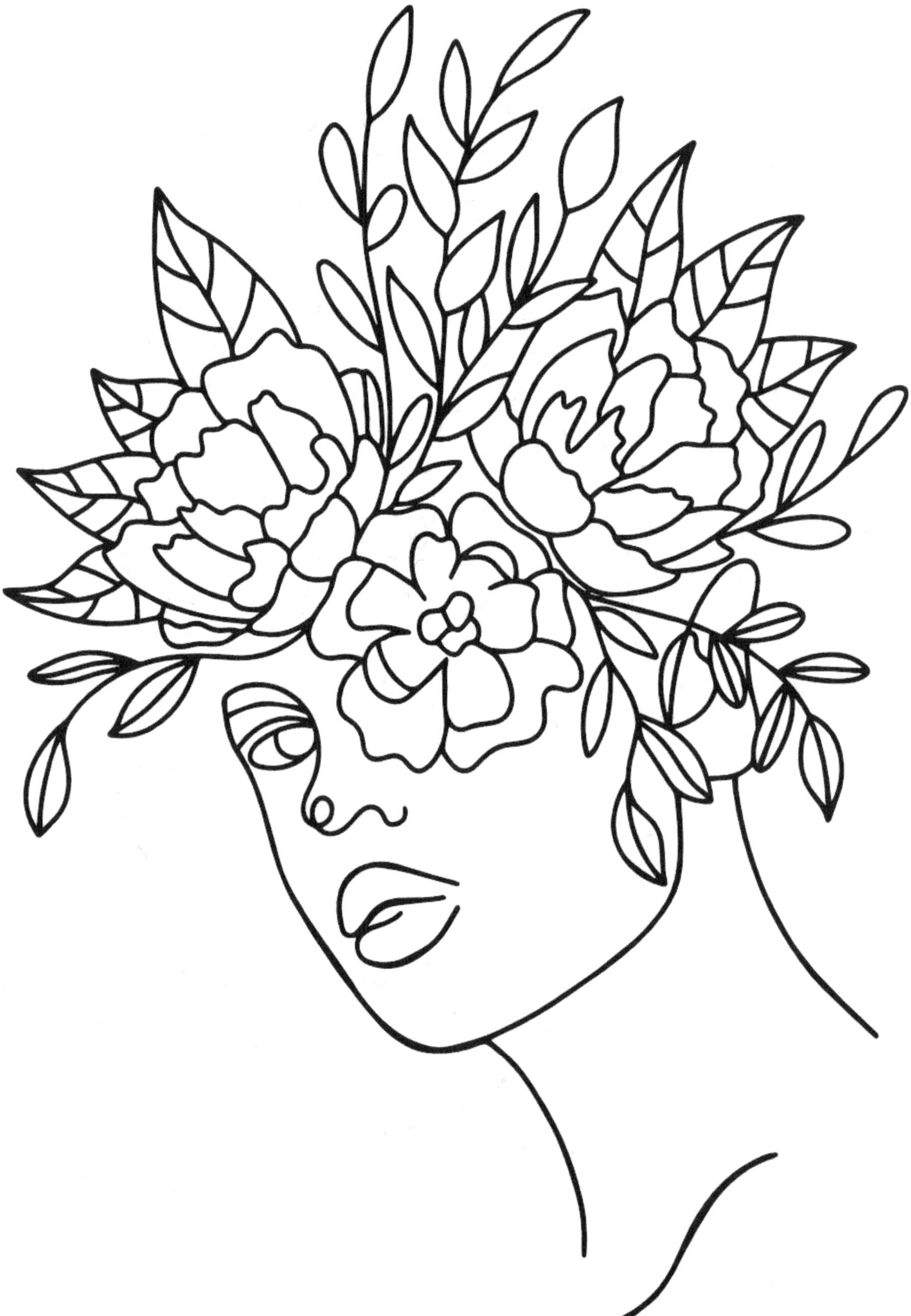

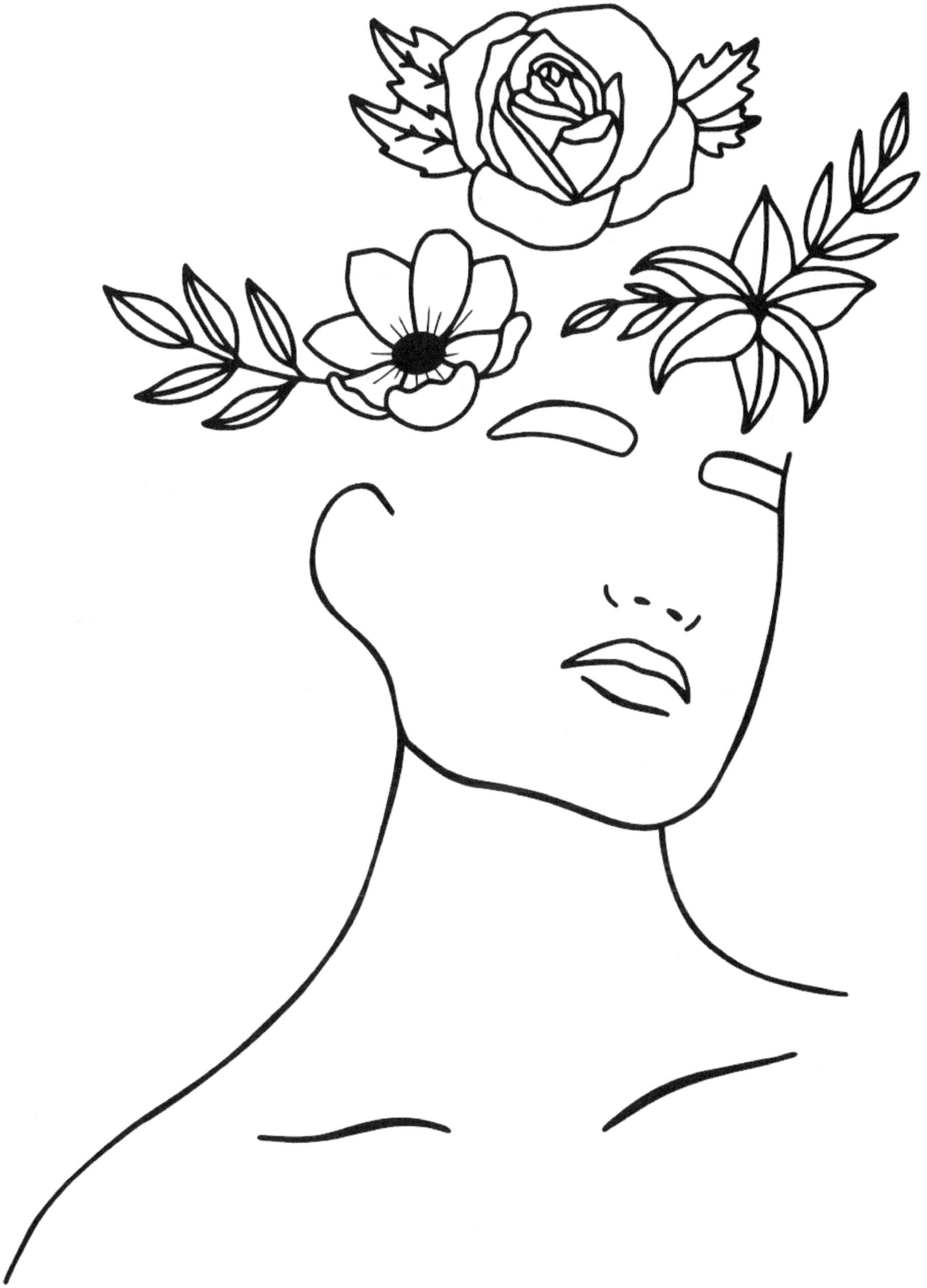

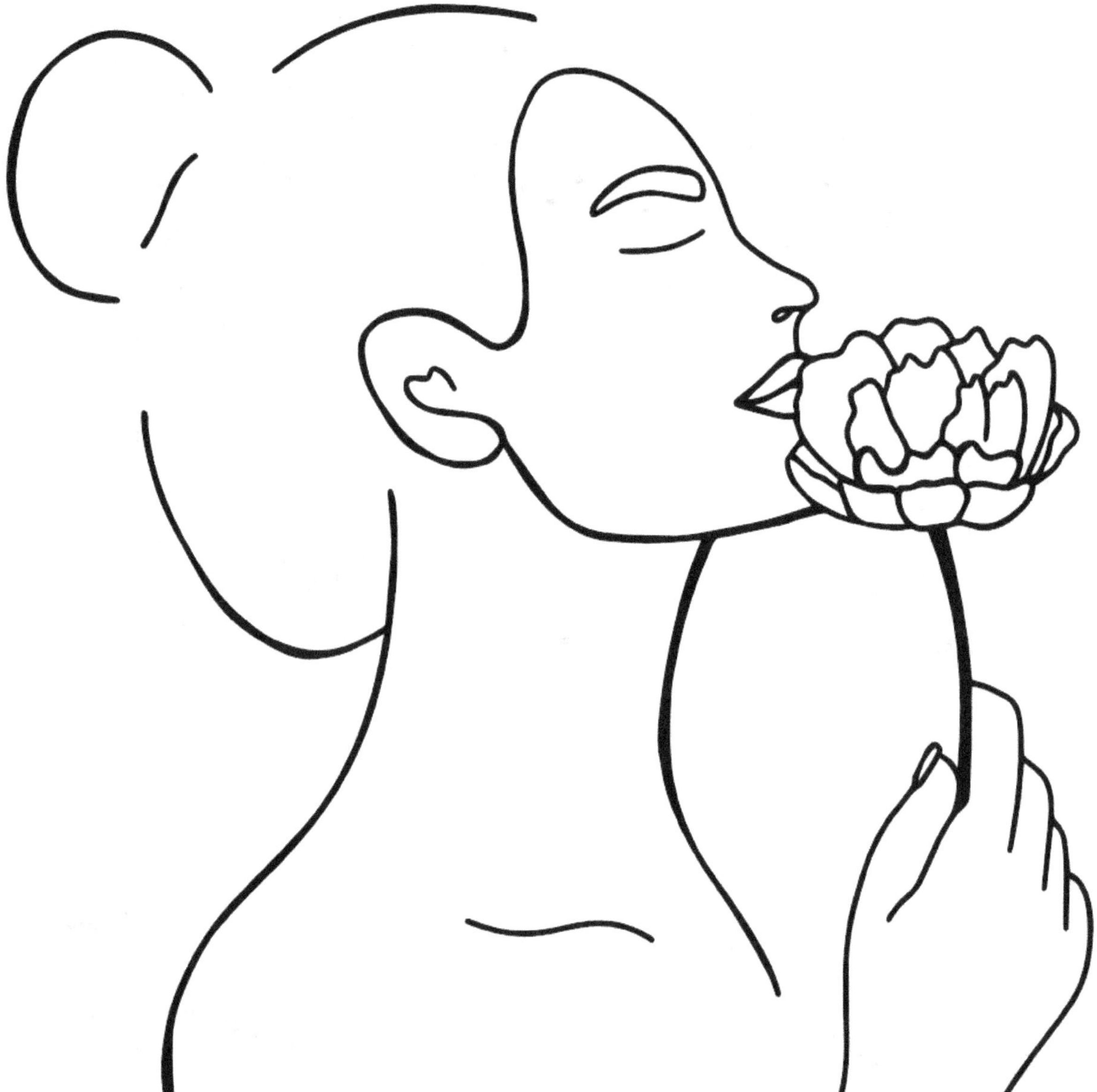

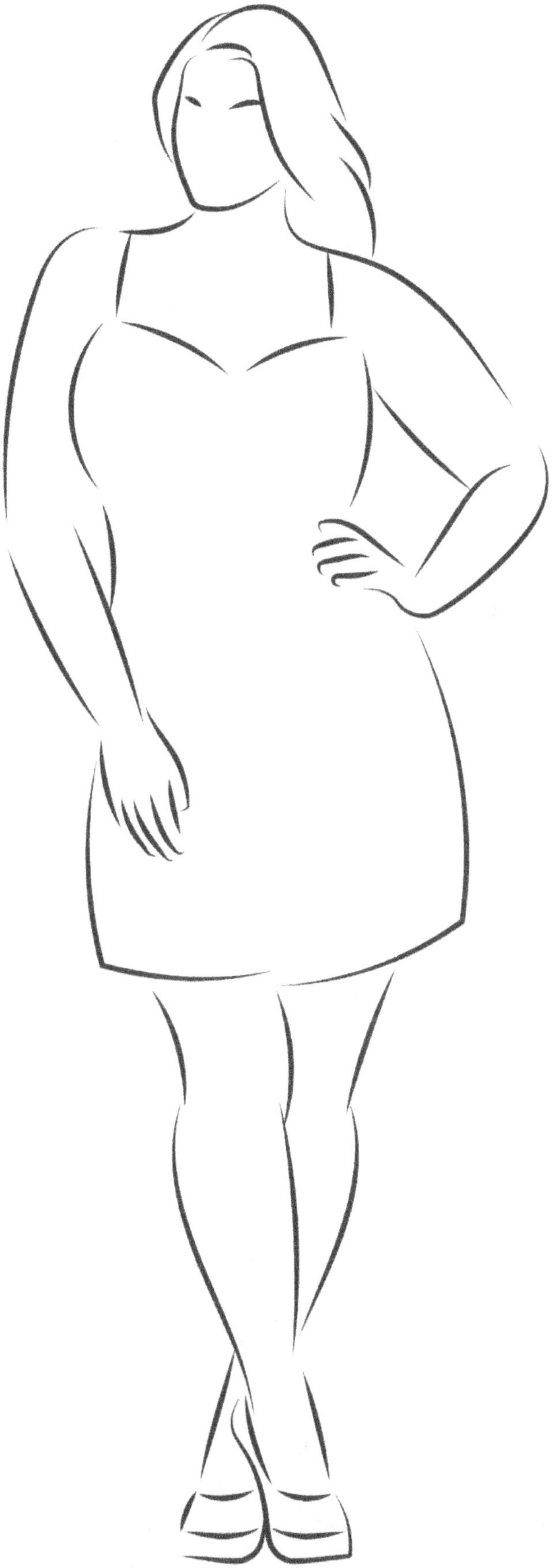

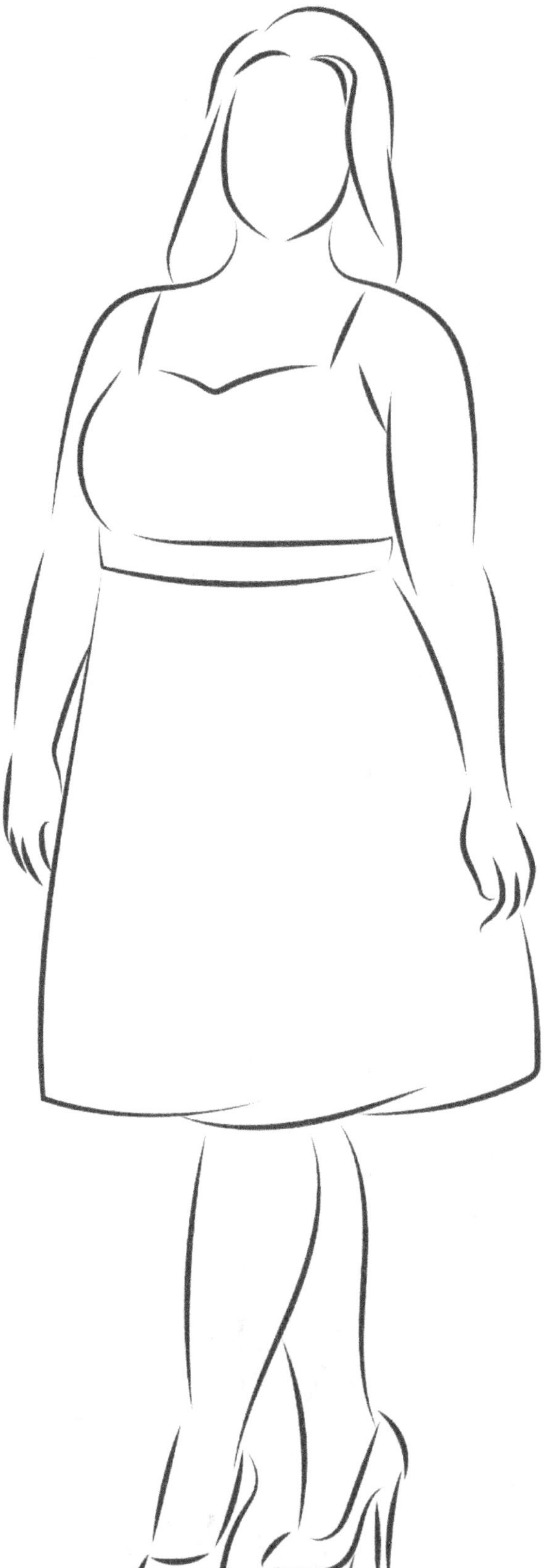

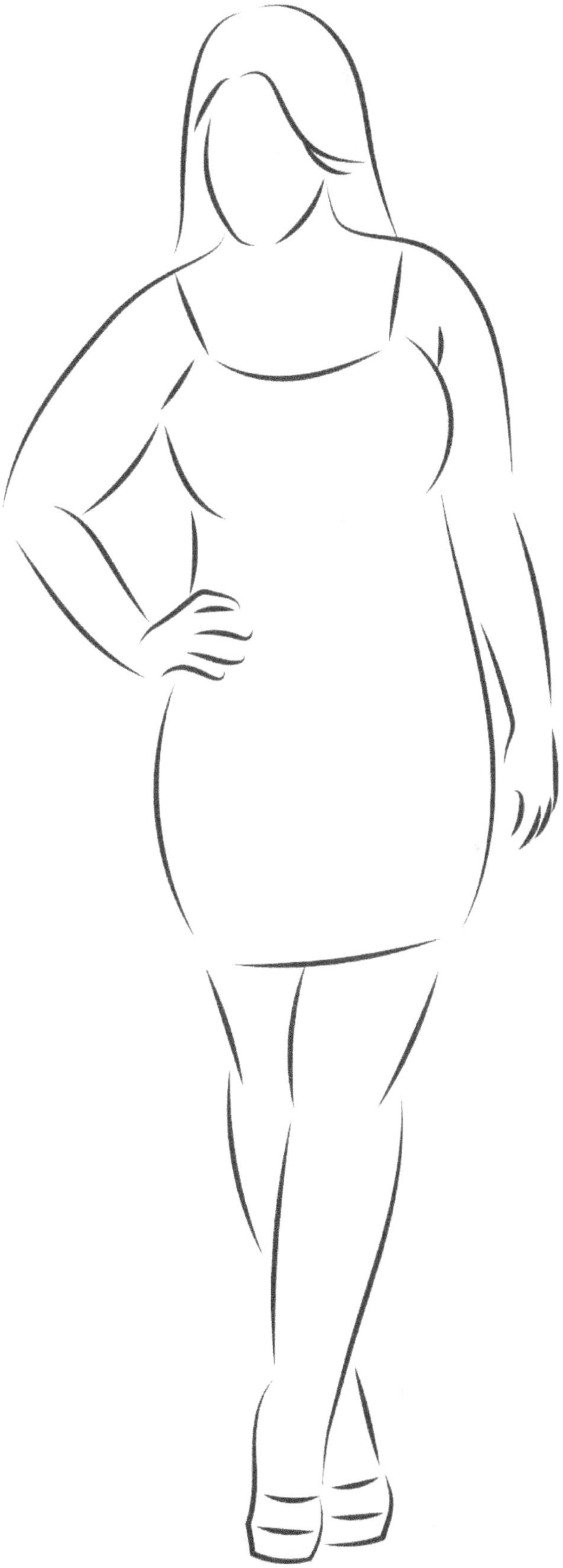

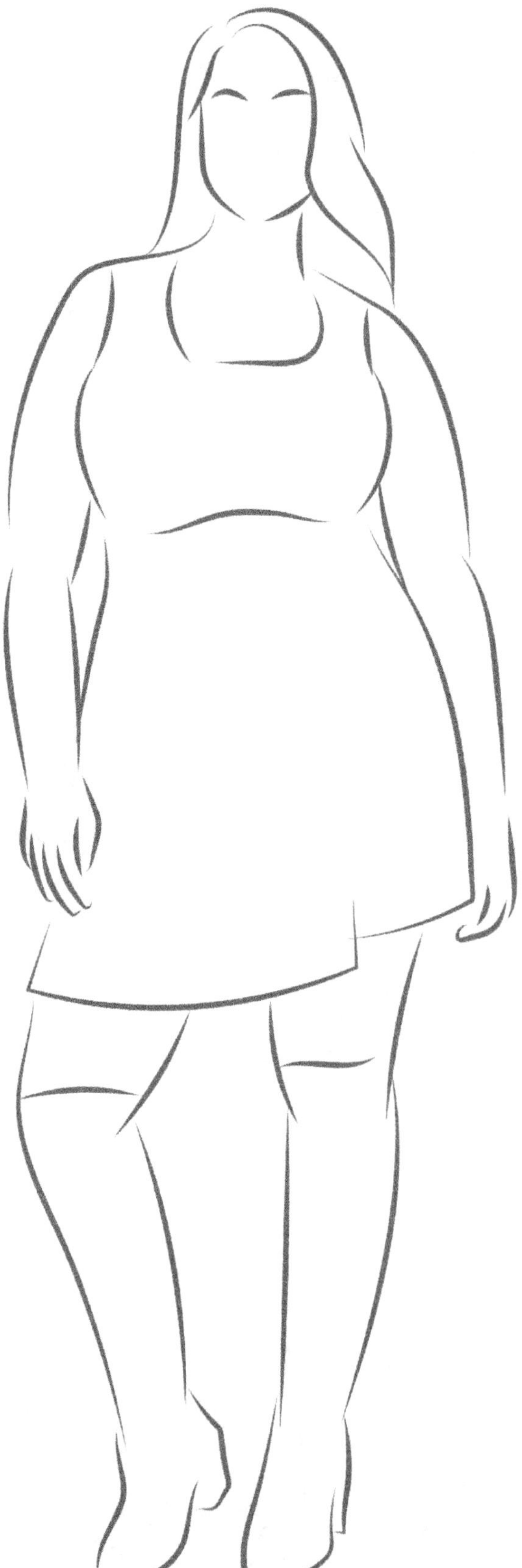

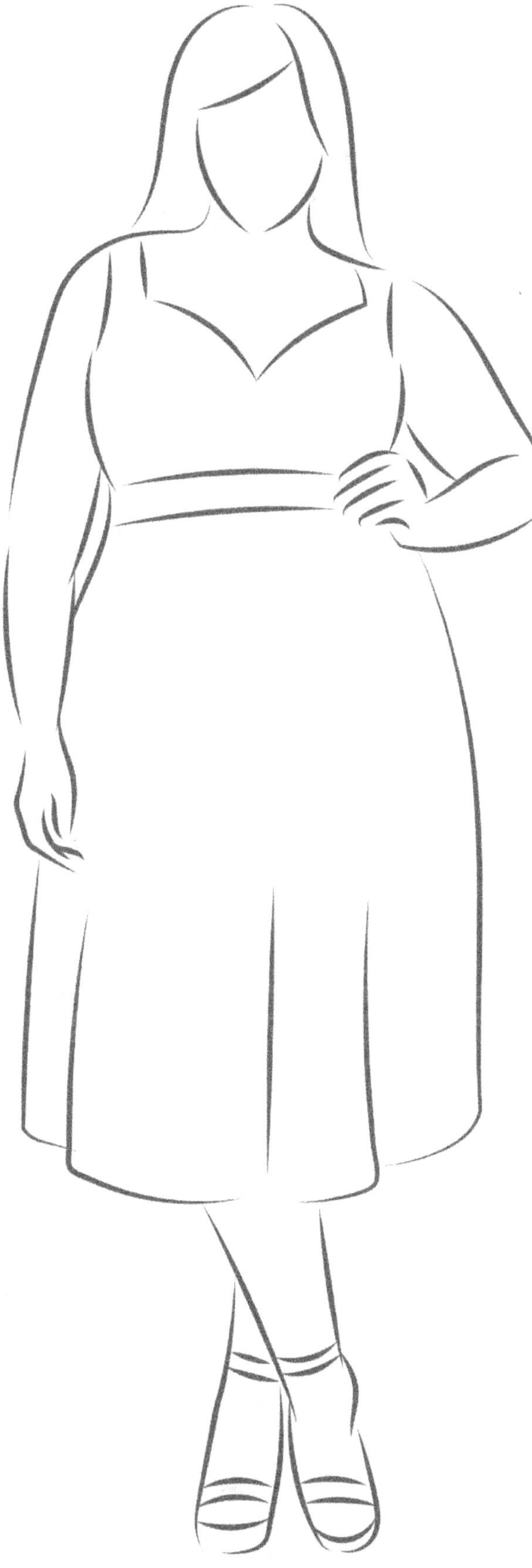

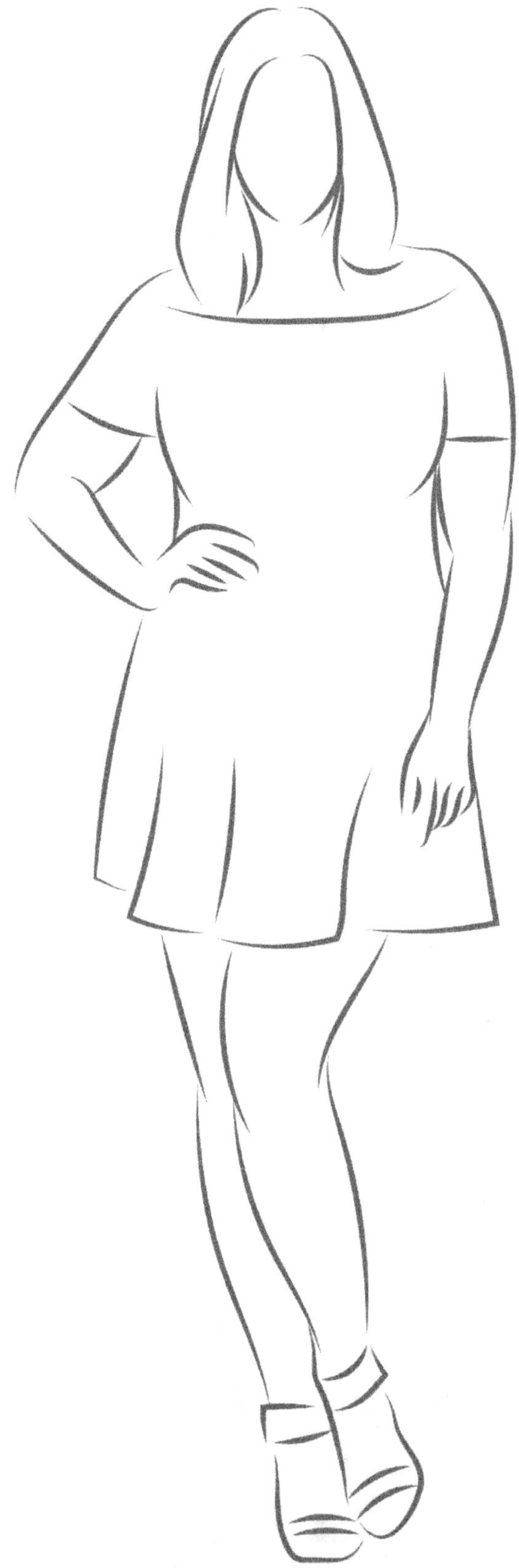

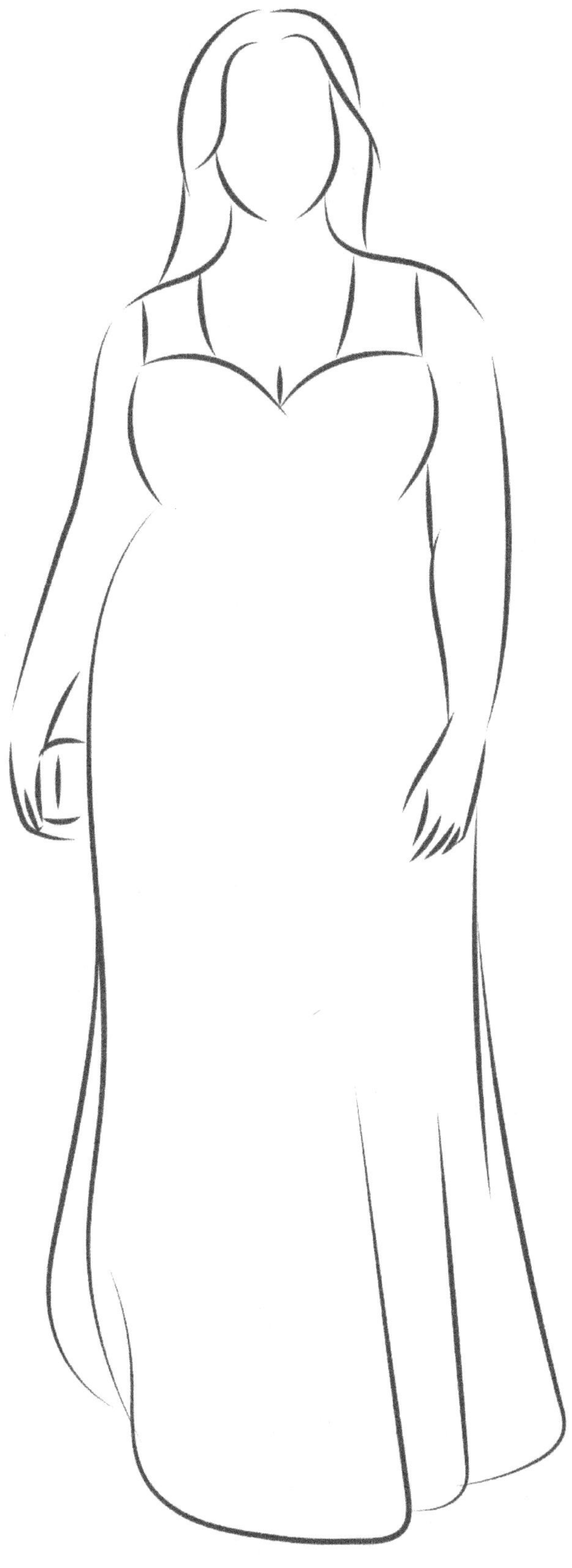

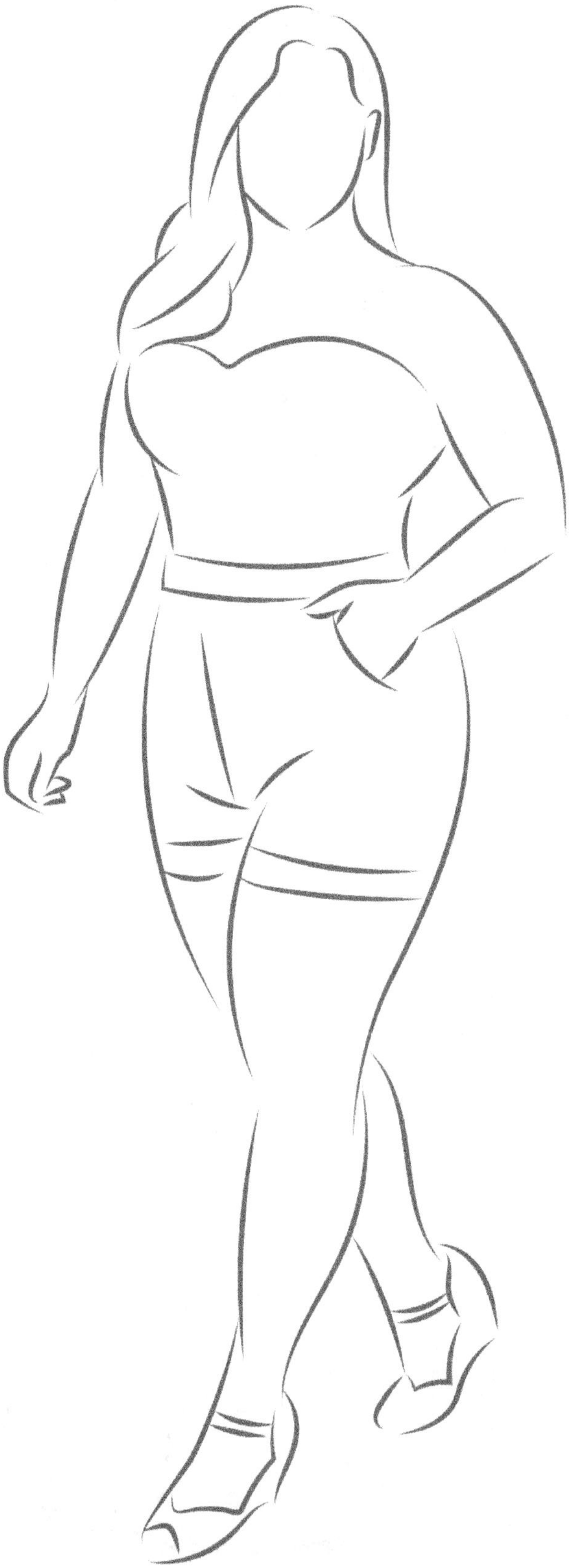

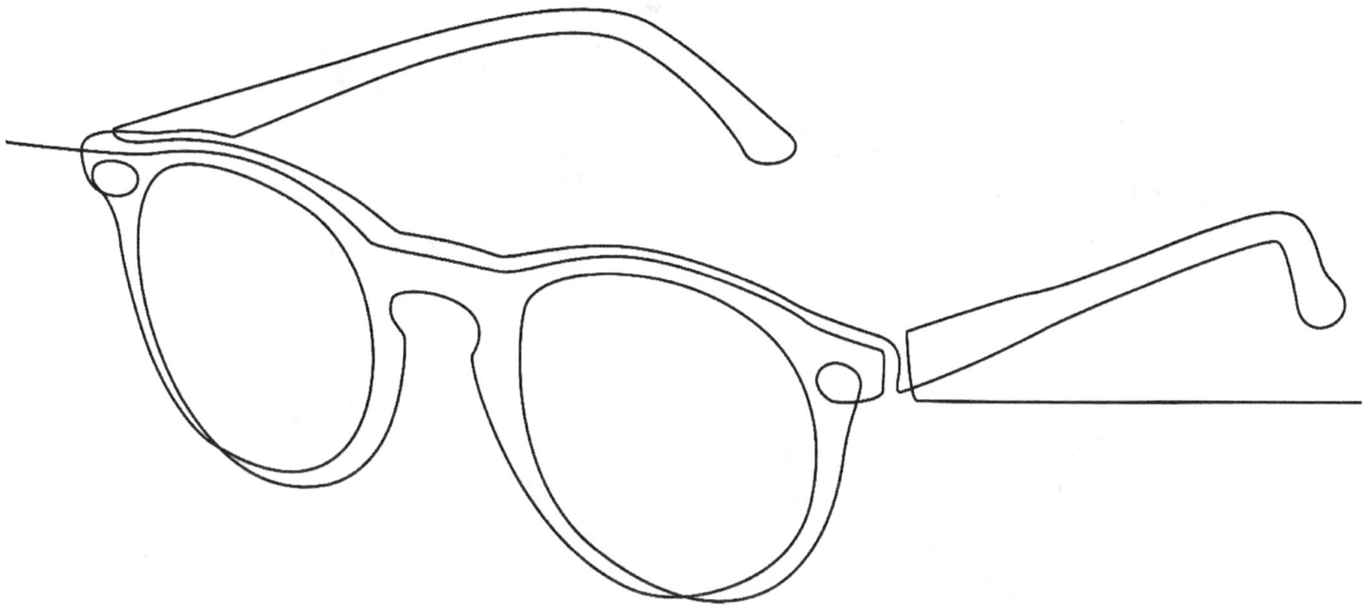

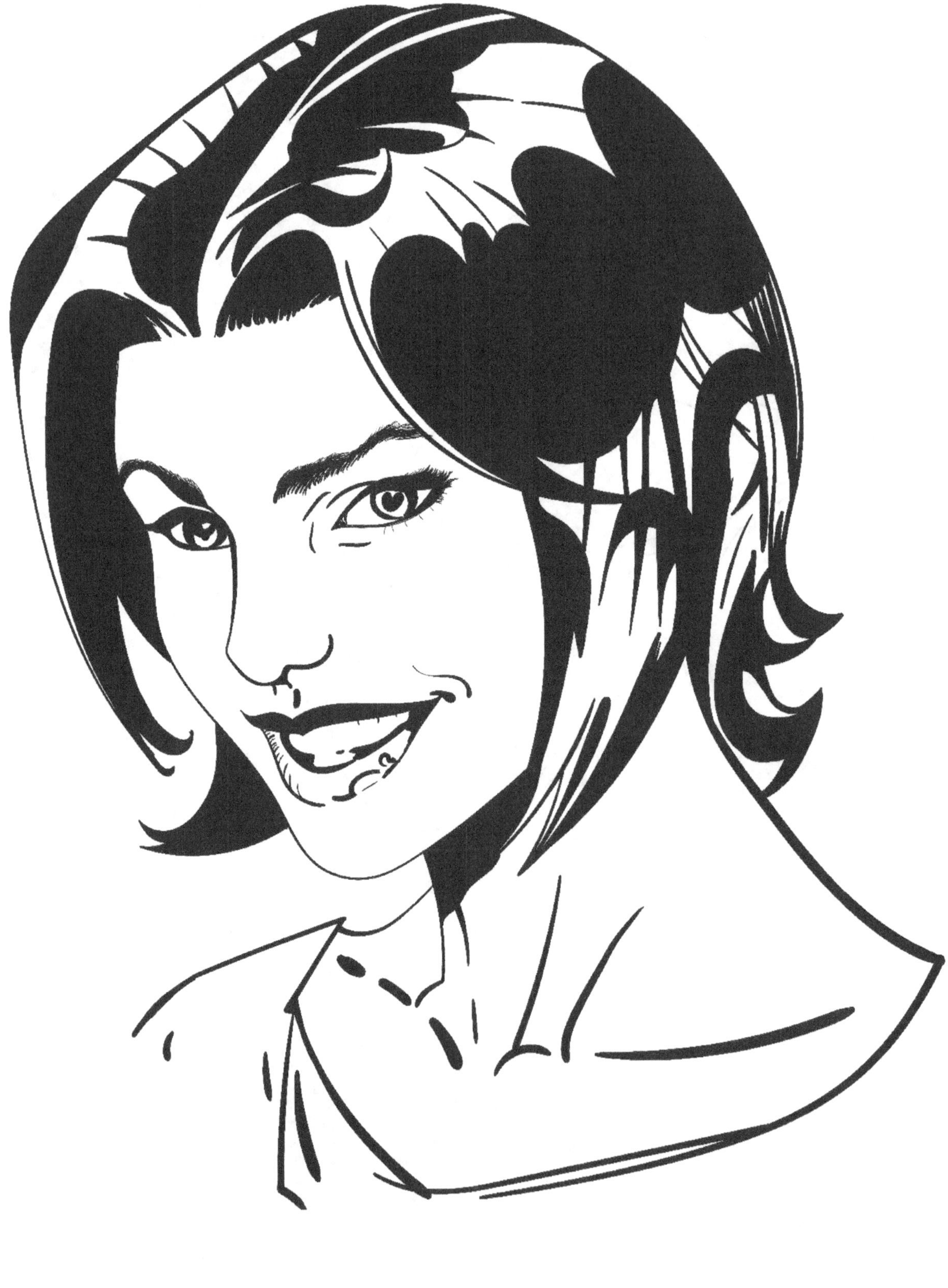

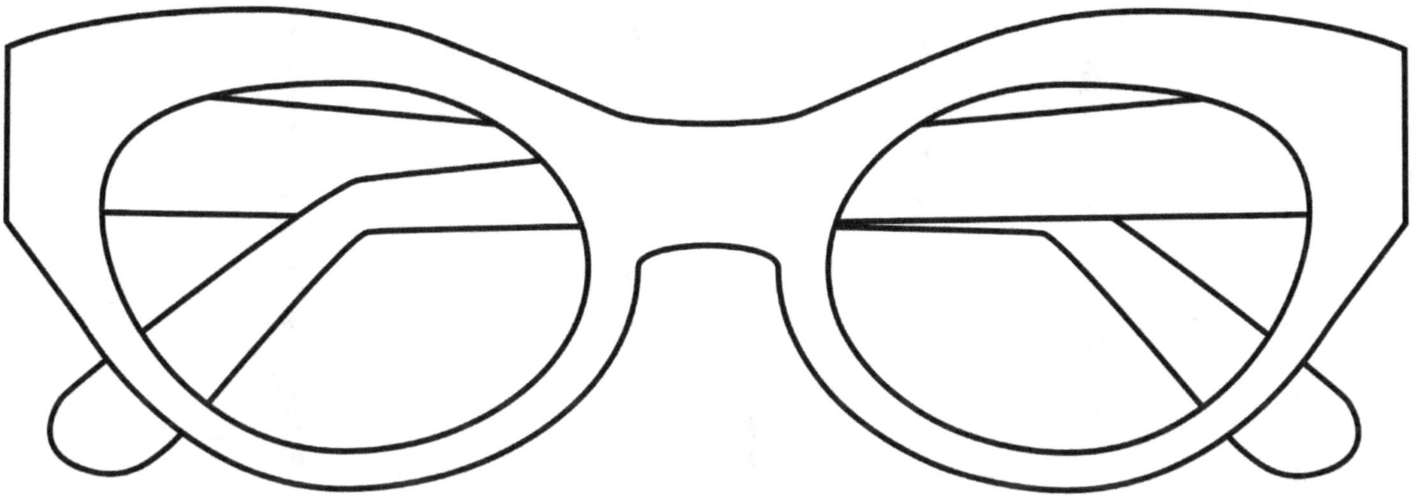

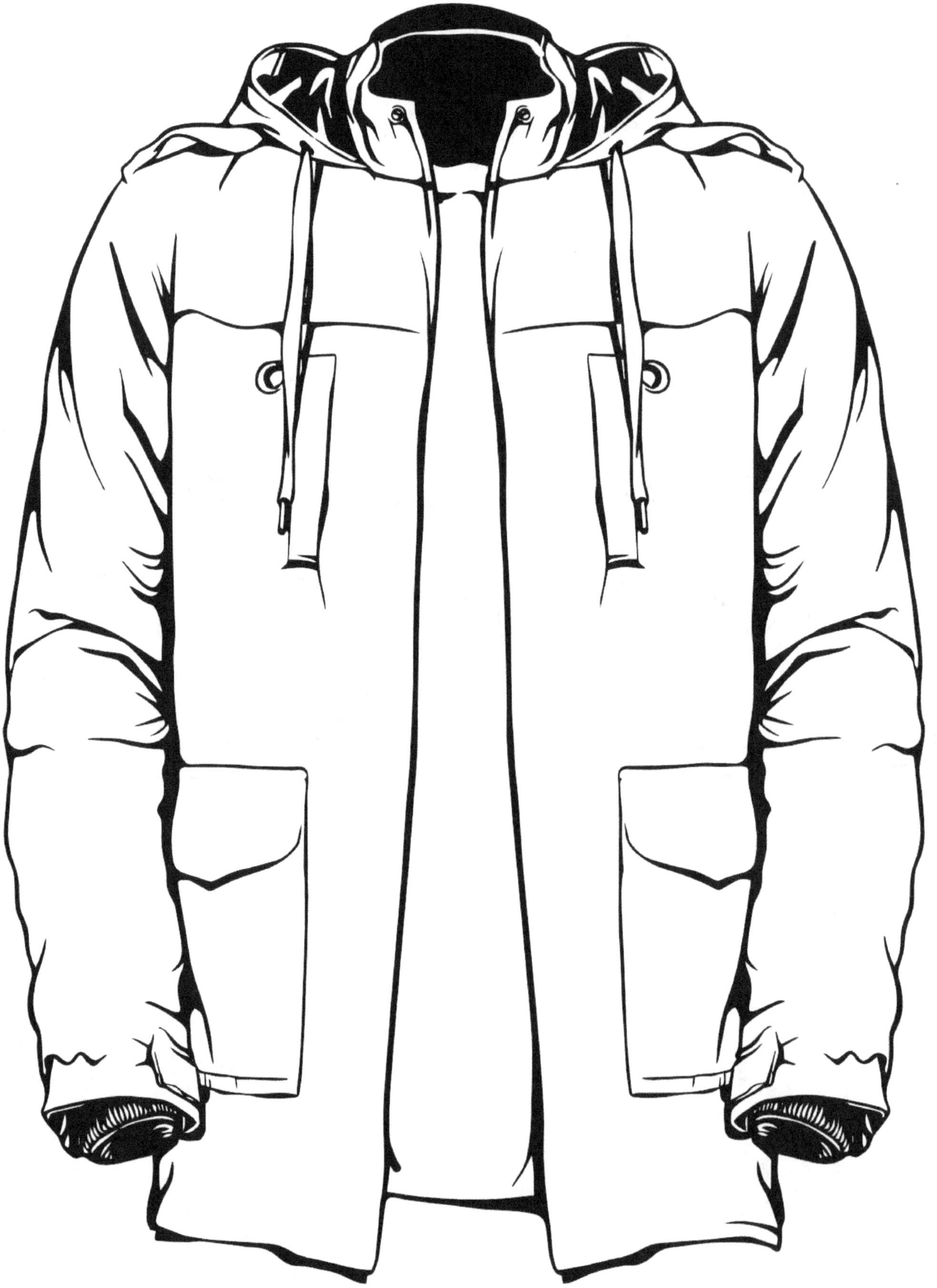

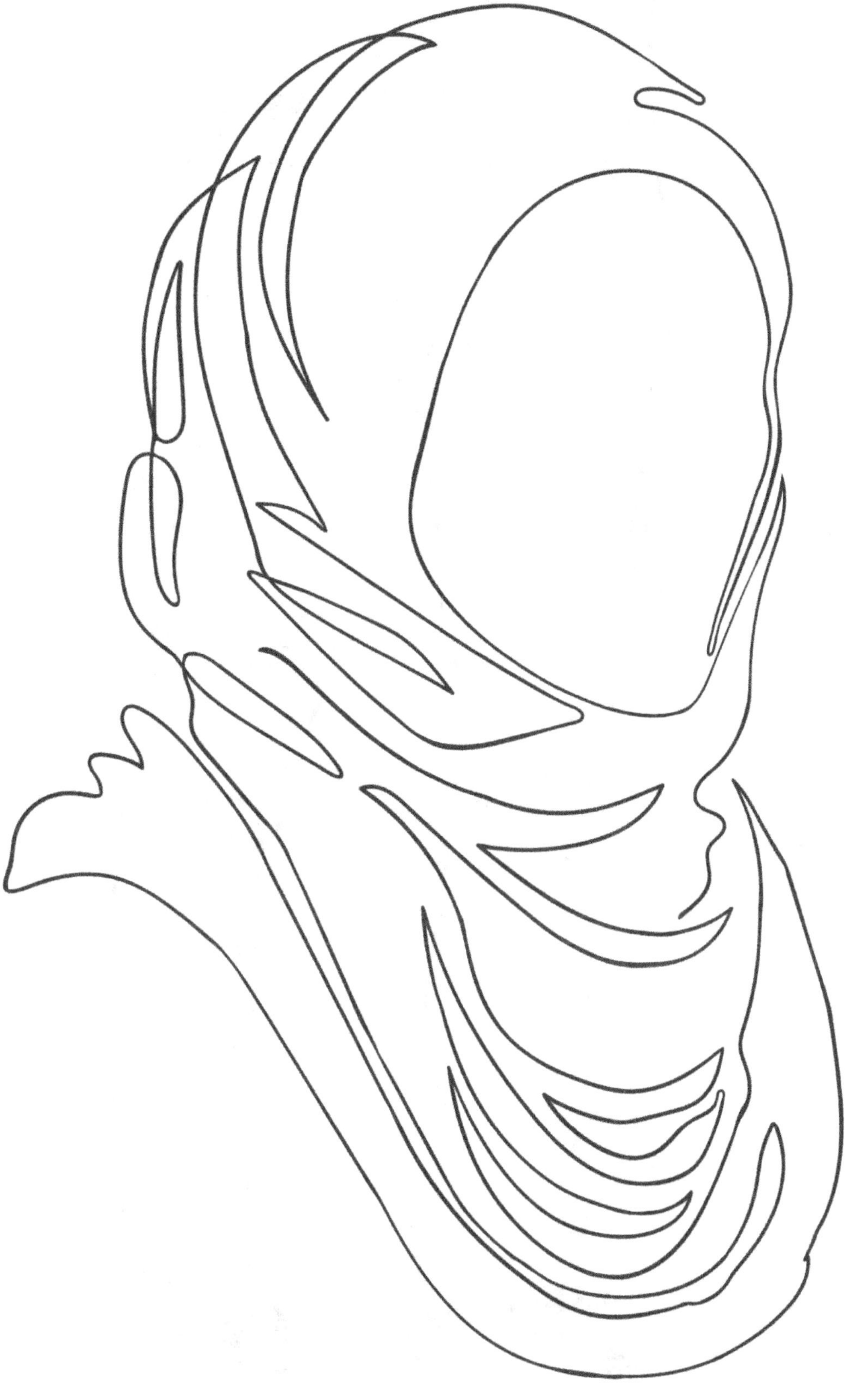

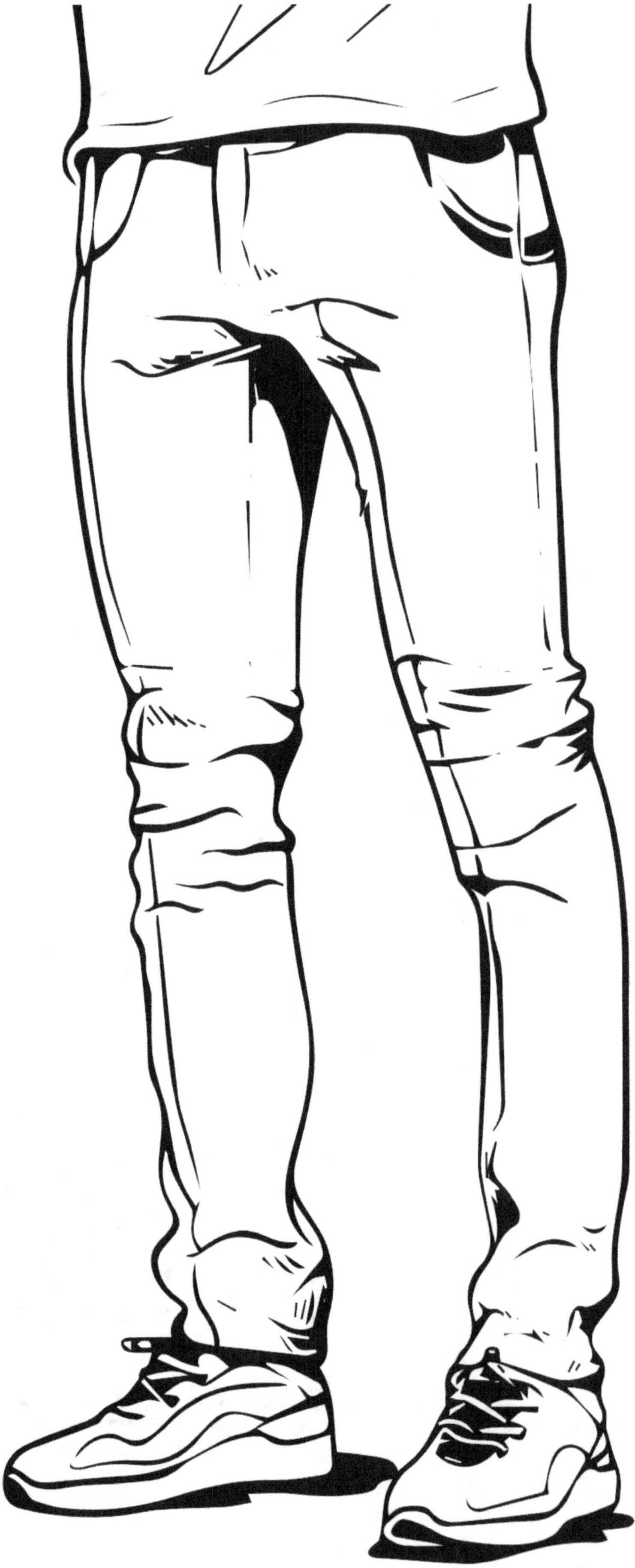

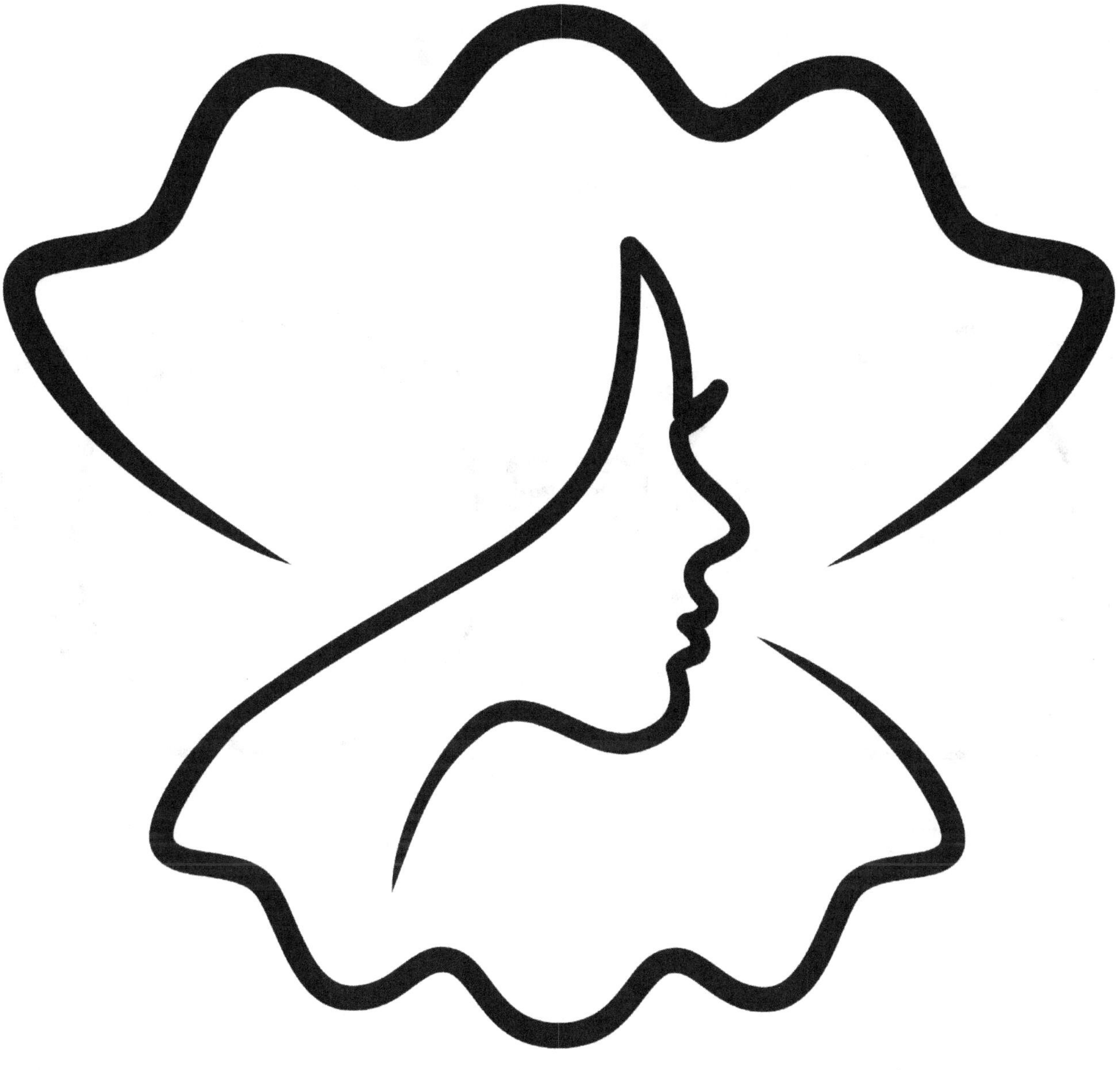

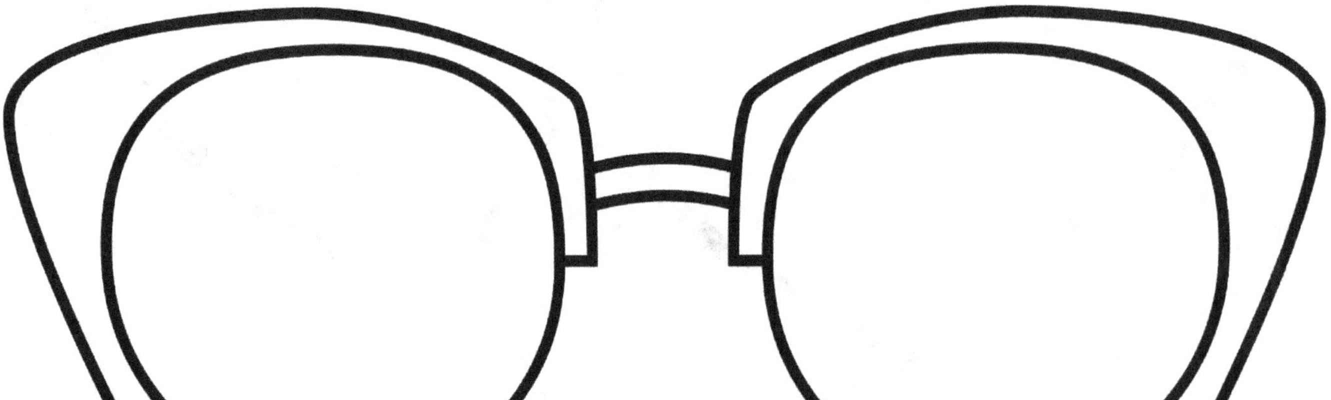

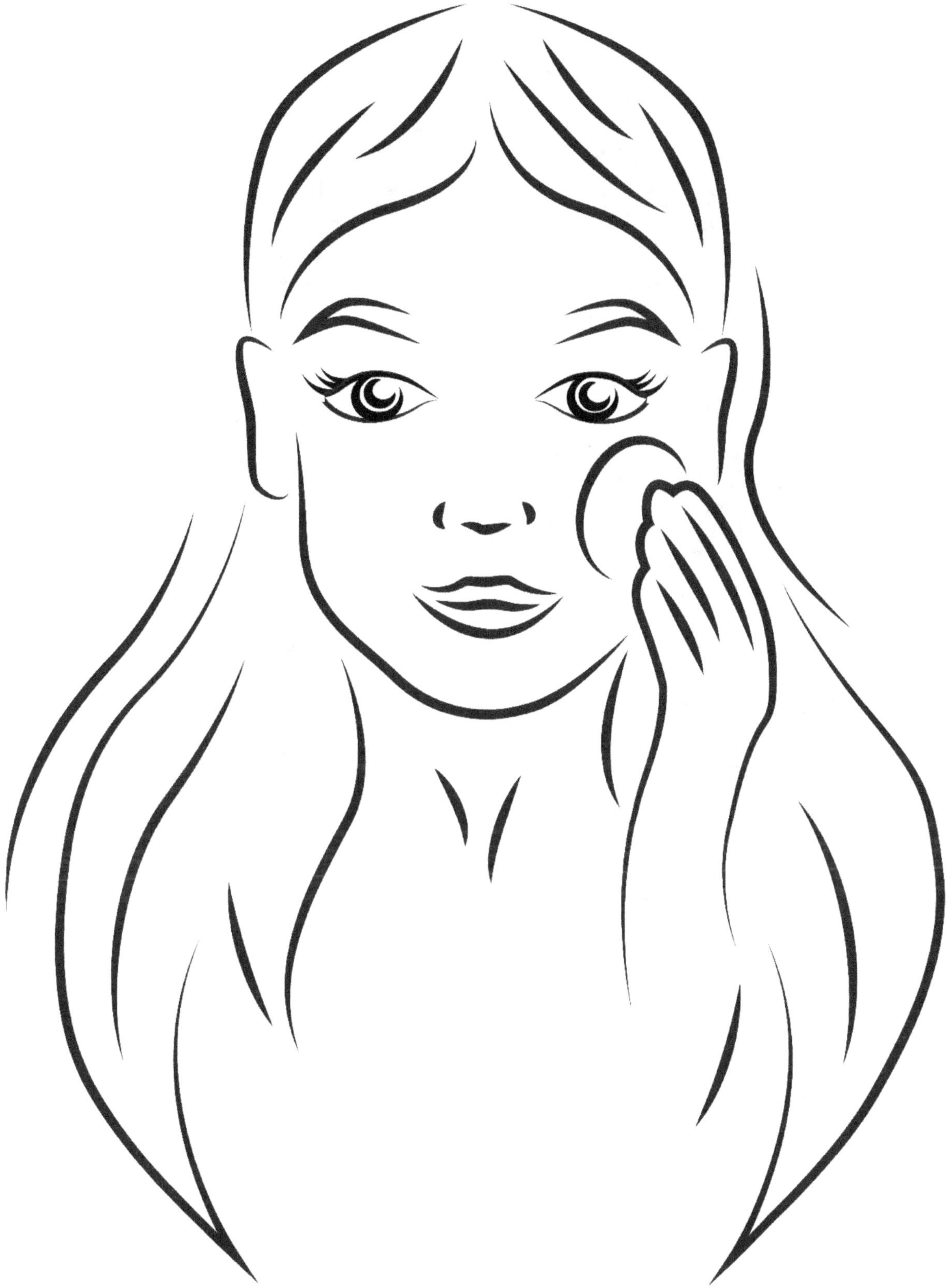

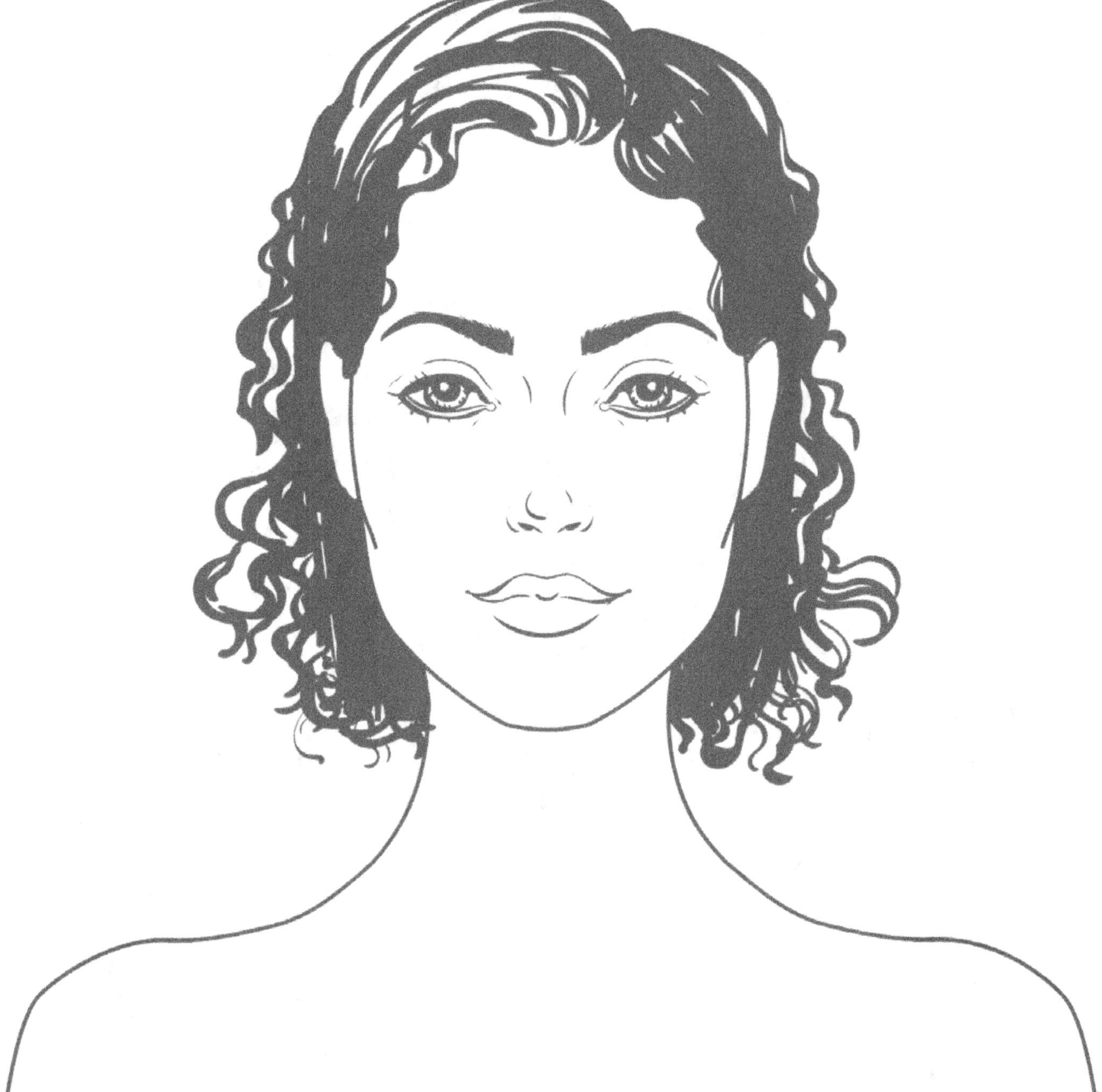

www.ingramcontent.com/pod-product-compliance
Lightning Source LLC
Chambersburg PA
CBHW081750220526
45468CB00008B/2313
9781794712300